AMERICA LOVES® SALADS

AMERICA LOVES® SALADS

101 All-Time Best Recipes

CAMILLE CUSUMANO

Illustrated by Judy Morgan

WINGS BOOKS
New York • Avenel, New Jersey

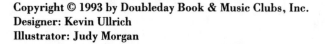

Copyright © 1993 by Doubleday Book & Music Clubs, Inc.
Designer: Kevin Ullrich
Illustrator: Judy Morgan

This 1994 edition is published by Wings Books,
distributed by Random House Value Publishing, Inc.,
40 Engelhard Avenue, Avenel, New Jersey 07001,
by arrangement with GuildAmerica Books®/Doubleday Book & Music
Clubs, Inc.

GuildAmerica Books® and America Loves® are registered trademarks
of Doubleday Book & Music Clubs, Inc.

AMERICA LOVES® SALADS was prepared and produced by
Michael Friedman Publishing Group, Inc.

Random House
New York • Toronto • London • Sydney • Auckland

Printed and bound in the United States of America

Library of Congress Cataloging-in-Publication Data

Cusumano, Camille.
    America loves salads/Camille Cusumano; illustrated by Judy
Morgan.
        p.   cm.
    Reprint. Originally published: Doubleday Book & Music Clubs.
    Includes index.
    ISBN 0-517-09379-0
    1. Salads,   I. Title.
TX740.C87 1993
 641.8' 3--dc20   93-8670
                                                       CIP

10 9 8 7 6 5 4 3 2

To Grace

ABOUT THE AUTHOR

Camille Cusumano is a cookbook author and editor, whose most recent works include *The New Foods: A Shopper's Guide with Recipes*. She worked for several years at Rodale Press, where she co-wrote *Rodale's Basic Natural Foods Cookbook* and wrote *Tofu, Tempeh, and Other Soy Delights*, as well as contributed to several health books. Her food and fitness articles have appeared in *The New York Times, Vegetarian Times, Attenzione*, and other national magazines and newspapers. Cusumano currently lives in San Francisco.

CONTENTS

INTRODUCTION

One spring day on a hike to the perfect picnic spot, some friends and I stumbled upon a fresh patch of miner's lettuce, a wild green that grows with abandon amid California's lush vegetation. The succulent emerald leaves coaxed us to make an early rest. I reached into my day pack and pulled out the cruet of vinaigrette that I had brought to embellish a later lunch dish. Everybody grabbed a fistful of leaves, the cruet was passed, and each one's handpicked greens (and hands) were dressed to taste.

This scene underscores the enduring pleasure of *herba salata,* or salted greens, as the Romans labeled the early salad. Civilization has elevated the salad to new heights, where those same rustic leaves of miner's lettuce may grace the most elegant menu imaginable today. Yet that rudimentary salad was the pinnacle of our day's feasting.

THE REBIRTH OF THE SALAD

Impromptu foraging aside, a lot has changed and a lot has stayed the same since humans first discovered wild edibles. The new American cuisine embraces salad, for it is a good way to experiment with new flavor combinations—with the "new" and ethnic ingredients that have entered our food markets and become more available to us as the world shrinks. Yet it is still a vehicle for the unadorned simplicity and innate goodness of nature. For salad has always been first and foremost a means of bringing garden (or farm) to table.

Some of the most toothsome of salads are still those composed of nothing more than the edible parts of herbs and plants, gently seasoned with the most basic of spices or a sprinkling of lemon juice or vinegar and oil. A salad, so versatile, can be as simple as fresh greens picked minutes before being heaped upon a plate or as elaborate as medallions of salmon suspended fancifully in a glistening aspic mold.

There are many new ways to compose and serve salads, yet old standards endure. The great American classics (Caesar Salad, Cobb Salad, for example) have not become obsolete by any means. Some may have even been improved nutritionally—relieved of high fat or salt content—or given new life with the addition of refreshing ingredients. And as we cultivate broader ethnic tastes, many new salads enter our mainstream repertoire, such as offerings from China, Japan, Thailand, and the countries of the Mediterranean.

Even the archetypal salad of iceberg lettuce is welcome on the American table today. The water-crisp, infinitely wilt-proof iceberg may have been out of favor for a while. But now it takes its place on a growing list of greatly varied salad bowl greens, mostly dark, each adding its own measure of earthy, peppery, bitter, sweet, mild, tangy, or grassy nuance. (Perhaps the mantle of gloppy bottle salad dressing that once dressed iceberg will never return from its deserved fall from grace.)

Our definition of salads has expanded. We find that salads go beyond the mere melange of raw ingredients. We now have cooked and warm salads. Salads may be based on a slice of grilled eggplant, a baked knob of goat cheese, or roasted peppers. And we can't resist embellishing with new things—a slice of daikon, an aromatic nut oil, or a few crumbs of imported blue-veined cheese.

THE CHANGING ROLE OF SALADS

When to serve salad is no longer narrowly defined as "between sweet and meat." Salads can whet the appetite, be the main event, offset a heavy meal, or cleanse the palate. Different salads can be served at various intervals of the meal. Gastronomical curiosity of recent years has also moved the salad around in the proverbial seven-course meal. A salad is not always light; indeed it can easily be pushed to extravagance or richness. So, it's not always served after the main course or before it, for that matter, it may be the main course or the full meal—or even the dessert. Most constraints are gone. You'll find salads in each section of this book that work well everywhere.

CHOOSING A SALAD

When choosing a salad, keep in mind the other elements of your menu. Fresh, tart greens will balance a rich, heavy meal. A more complex salad of several ingredients will complement a lighter meal. Potato salads, a Waldorf salad, bean and mayo-dressed salads are generally informal, good picnic fare (and some elegant salads travel well to outdoor feasts). All options are included here with many suggestions for how to use them.

Salads can be as visually appealing and soothing to look at as a bouquet of flowers. There is color, texture, and shape, which you can embellish with a deft knife or clever arrangement. Buffet spreads can be set with eye-appealing salads of every sort: molds, filled vegetable containers, marinated vegetables, and decoratively garnished salad platters. Your own imagination will no doubt build upon the suggestions offered.

The main theme of any salad, simple or elaborate, is to uphold the natural goodness, that sometimes elusive quality called freshness. Optimal freshness is the hallmark of a successful salad. The savvy salad chef also knows that the dressing can make or break a good medley of ingredients and always errs on the side of frugality when dressing a salad. The last chapter of this book discusses dressings and their basic components—oils and vinegars—offering guidelines for pairing them with different salads. Other than these basic tenets, salads encourage creativity and can be molded to personal taste. The recipes that follow are offered as a jumping-off point. Feel free to experiment and tailor them to meet your own definition of successful salad making.

Chapter One

GREEN AND VEGETABLE SALADS

The mixed green salad has always had lyrical simplicity. Now that simplicity has infinitely more shade and nuance—leaves can be dark green or light, ruby red; curled, furled, frizzy, wavy, or flat; bitter, sharp, mellow, bland, or sweet. They can be delicate and mild or so pungent and peppery they seem to bite the tongue. Developing an educated palate—by tasting all the various greens and recognizing their idiosyncrasies—is the only way to mix them effectively. A good way to sample them all is to sprinkle them just until they glisten with a simple vinaigrette, say one part white wine vinegar to two parts olive or nut oil. You will quickly find the balance of mild and robust greens that suits your taste.

Vegetables, too, are one of the most basic foundations of classic salads. More alchemy can be worked with the tastes, textures, colors, and shapes of the vegetable kingdom than with just about any other group of ingredients. Often a salad dressing will act as a marinade, "cooking" the vegetable to bring forth its best attributes.

GREENS GLOSSARY

Although greens each have their own unique, sometimes indescribable, flavor, for simplicity's sake, it is easiest to divide them generally into mild and assertive categories. Some people like a balance of strong and mild in their salad, while others may prefer all mild or all assertive greens. Whichever taste you have, just make sure the greens are very fresh. It doesn't take much experience to tell a crackling fresh green from a tired, wilted one. When choosing your greens, check for any decay or brown spots, especially near the stem base, where the lettuce was picked, or if possible near the center of the head, where deterioration may be hidden.

The mild greens include:

Butterhead. Smaller, less compact, loosely packed, delicate, "buttery" flavored leaves. Includes **butter, Boston, limestone,** and **Bibb.** Holds dressing well. Combines well with loose-leaf, watercress, radicchio, spinach, or endive.

Iceberg. Crisp, crunchy, tightly packed. Does not wilt easily. Blends well with all greens.

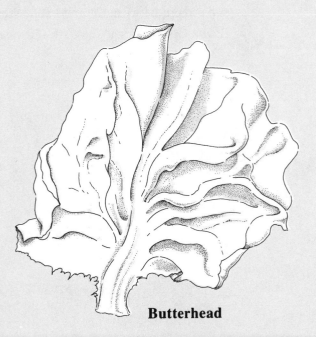

Butterhead

Loose-leaf. Tender, mellow, and soft. Can be solid green (greenleaf) or have red-tinged (ruby or redleaf) edges. It is loosely bunched, fragile lettuce. Makes a pretty platter liner for molds and other salads. Shape of the smooth varieties may resemble that of a large oak leaf. Some have frilly, more ruffled edges. Includes **leaf, oakleaf, redleaf,** and **greenleaf.** Goes well with arugula, radicchio, watercress, or romaine.

Mâche. Also called **corn salad** or **lamb's lettuce.** Highly perishable. Grows in corn fields. It is sweet, highly coveted, usually expensive. Best served alone or with a few edible flowers.

Romaine. This elongated head with crisp, stiff leaves, generally dark green, is somewhere between the mild and assertive greens, with a pleasant sweet grassy flavor. Goes well with butterhead, watercress, loose-leaf, or arugula.

Romaine

The assertive greens include:

Arugula. Also called **rocket** and **roquette.** Very lively bite, very peppery and nutty, can be bitter, has an unmistakable pine-scent herby aroma. Has long frayed leaves, emerald in color. Best served alone when not too pungent. Also blends well with loose-leaf, radicchio, butterhead, and spinach.

Belgian endive. A cold-weather vegetable that starts out as escarole, but then becomes a furled bunch of blanched leaves when the farmer sequesters the plants in total darkness for a while. This natural bleaching deprives the leaves of the light-dependent green chlorophyll of plant life. The pigment-deprived leaves are tender yet crisp. The inner hearts are especially favored for their clean, bitterish flavor. Blends well with arugula, radicchio, butterhead, or watercress.

Arugula

Belgian endive

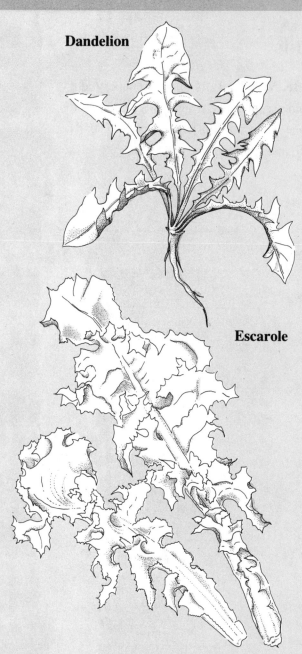

Dandelion

Escarole

Dandelion. Also a bitter green, its French name *dent de lion* (lion's teeth) refers to its jagged-edged leaves that somewhat resemble curly endive but are less fleshy. Use raw or cooked. Good with a mix of other bitter and sweet greens such as arugula or watercress. Good in wilted salads with hot dressings. Smaller heads are best, less bitter and more tender. Blends well with butterhead, loose-leaf, or iceberg.

Escarole. Also called **chicory escarole.** A winter vegetable that is a bitter leafy green. Can be eaten raw or cooked as a vegetable. Escarole is a flat-leafed cousin of **curly chicory** (curly endive, or *frisée*). Escarole's leaves are fleshier, greener, flatter, while those of curly chicory are narrow and spinier, with curly serrated edges. Both types have a lighter yellow inner heart due to a blanching method used in the fields where the greens are grown. Goes well with loose-leaf, butterhead, and other mild lettuces.

Mizuna. A member of the mustard family that resembles chicory, but with a longer stem. Leaves vary from light to dark green, and taste is bitter and pungent. Goes well with butterhead, watercress, radicchio, or arugula.

Sorrel. Also called **sour grass.** Contains the compound oxalate potash, which lends the characteristic sharp, sour taste. Has deep clover green leaves and is often grown in hothouses. Its arrowhead-shaped leaves wilt quickly, but this potherb retains distinct sharpness. It is often cooked and made into a sauce or cream soup. Add it in small amounts to salads with sweeter and mellow greens. Combines well with sweet or mild lettuces, such as butterhead or loose-leaf.

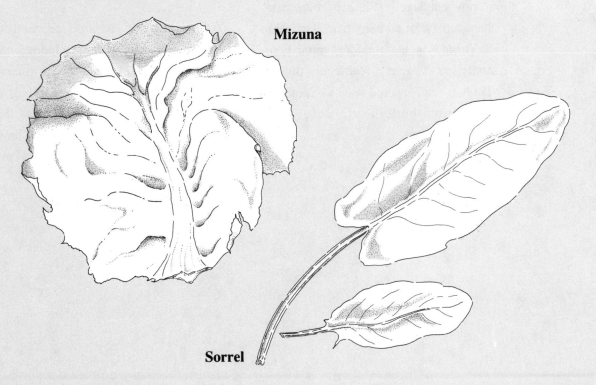

Mizuna

Sorrel

Spinach. With its mild, faintly grassy taste, spinach has become a quite familiar salad ingredient. Its flavor is somewhere between mild and assertive. The dark, pine-green spinach (known by **Bloomsdale** and other names) with the thicker leaves is good in salads, but not as delicate and sprightly flavored as the **New Zealand** spinach, with its emerald green, flatter, and more tender leaves. **Flatleaf spinach** is also good in salads. Combines well with any mild or assertive flavored greens.

Radicchio. Brilliant striated mauve-and-ivory leaves. Leaves are as stiff and crisp as raw cabbage. Pleasant bitterness, characteristic of all chicories. **Radicchio di Verona** is the rounder, more commonly found variety. **Radicchio di Treviso** has long, tapered leaves. Combines well with butterhead, loose-leaf, arugula, or endive.

MESCLUN SALAD MIX

You may see, at the produce stand, a salad mix of various greens including many of those mentioned here. To be a true mesclun mix, it should include just baby, or young, lettuces. The French name comes from the mix of tender young lettuces that have been harvested and sold at Paris farmers' markets.

Radicchio

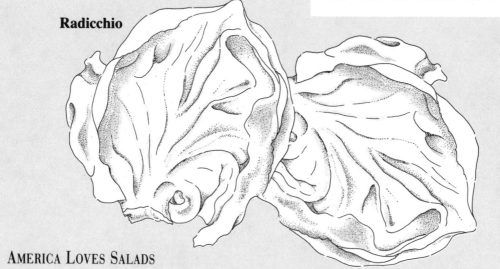

Watercress. With dime-sized leaves on juicy stems, it has an earthy, herblike flavor. Can be pureed into a tangy dressing. Use the tender part of stems as well as the leaves in salads. Goes well with iceberg, butterhead, loose-leaf or endive.

UNUSUAL OR WILD GREENS

You may encounter any of the following in the wild or at specialty markets:

Amaranth greens. This ancient Aztec food was out of favor for centuries. The raw greens are rich in calcium and iron. It tastes mildly like spinach, with a more assertive pepperiness. Its leaves are pretty—maroon-tinged emerald green.

Fiddlehead ferns. These plumed green swirls are ostrich fern shoots picked at an early stage of development. They have a nutty, wheatgrass flavor and are a dearly priced gourmet item.

Miner's lettuce, purslane, borage, burnet, red clover. All great salad bowl ingredients, most often found in the wild. If you are lucky enough to find them, use them soon after picking. Like most wild greens, each has its own unique, generally assertive, earthy flavor.

USING RAW VEGETABLE GREENS

Kale, beet greens, mustard greens, Swiss chard, bok choy, and the cabbages—including red, green, napa, and savoy—are all great additions, adding flavor and often texture to salad.

HERBS

Several fresh herbs can be added right to the salad bowl along with the greens. Be sure to wash and dry them well and chop or julienne them for better dispersal throughout the salad. These fresh herbs are especially good: basil, chervil, parsley, cilantro, sage, mint, oregano, tarragon. In general, when using herbs this way in a salad, add only one type.

FLOWERS

The petals or blossoms of flowers added to salads may surprise you with a splash of color and burst of flavor. Add just a few, maybe one to two blossoms per serving. Most flowers have somewhere between a peppery, lemony tart, or pleasantly bitter taste. Roses, calendulas, daylilies, nasturtiums, geraniums, marigolds, violets, chrysanthemums, and borage blossoms are the most commonly used. Make sure the flowers are not sprayed. Don't eat any flower unless you are sure it is not poisonous. If you gather your own, it is said that morning, when they are still awash in dew, is the best time. Handle them gently, for they bruise all too easily.

ORGANIC PRODUCE

Organically grown produce often tastes better—even if it does not look better. It is generally defined as produce that is grown without the use of synthetic fertilizers, pesticides, herbicides, preservatives, colorings, or radiation. Requirements may vary from state to state. Call your state department of agriculture for more information.

TEMPERATURE OF SALADS

I recommend that most salads be served at room temperature. Not long ago it was fashionable to chill mixed salads in the freezer until just before serving them. I believe this chills away flavor. If you like an ice-chilled salad, you can trust your own palate and eat it that way.

SOME TIPS ON GREENS-BASED SALADS:

• In general, limit to three the number of ingredients in addition to the greens.

• Use thick creamy-type dressings on thick-textured greens such as iceberg or romaine. Use lighter vinaigrettes on soft greens.

• Add juicy ingredients such as tomatoes, cucumbers, and oranges or other fruits just before tossing and serving the salad to avoid wilting the greens.

• Never cut greens with a knife, as this encourages oxidation and cuts off flavor at the edge. Always tear them to desired size.

• If you make the salad a while before it is to be served, try this for convenience and to preserve optimum freshness: Thoroughly mix the salad dressing in the bottom of the bowl; then place all the salad mixings on top, but *do not toss* until just before serving. Do this no longer than a half hour in advance.

• Make sure all ingredients, including the greens, are thoroughly dry after washing. Residual moisture will dilute your dressing and keep it from adhering to vegetables.

• Nutritional tip: Although some salads suggest using the inner light-colored leaves, usually for aesthetic reasons, bear in mind that the darker outer leaves are richer in calcium, iron, and vitamin A.

WASHING AND STORING GREENS

Some greens remain crisp longer than others. The best advice is to use all greens as you buy—or pick—them. Most greens—iceberg and romaine are exceptions—begin to wilt in a day or so.

Never wash greens before storing them; moisture encourages wilting. To protect leafy greens from moisture already on them, wrap them in a few layers of paper toweling, then in perforated (or open-ended) plastic. Store them in the vegetable crisper of the refrigerator.

To clean greens: If they are tightly packed, break the leaves away from the bunch at the basal stalk and rinse them under running water or in a basin full of water. Rinse well to remove stubborn grit and bugs.

Dry them thoroughly: After the food processor, the lettuce spin-dryer has been the best kitchen invention in recent times. It's cheap and the most effective way to remove every last drop of moisture from greens. The only other way is to drain them in a colander for a while, then pat them dry with paper towel, but this takes enough work and time to discourage even the most fervent of cooks.

THE WELL-SEASONED SALAD BOWL

A well-seasoned salad bowl is a good thing to have if you are a regular salad eater. I find that the best salad bowls are big and somewhat shallow, as opposed to deep ones, which allow ingredients to weigh upon each other too much. It may be made of olive, walnut, mahogany, or maple wood. Ceramic and glass bowls are fine, too, though, not being porous material, they won't hold the seasoning the way wood will.

It is mainly the aromatic flavors of garlic and some herbs that will linger and add to each successive salad tossed in a wooden bowl. With time you will learn how much garlic-control to exercise, depending on your own tolerance or taste. You will also see that garlic in the dressing is somehow different from garlic rubbed into the bowl.

Rub the bowl with the cut side of a clove of garlic each time you make a salad. After a while you may find this step unnecessary as enough garlic flavor and aroma will remain in the porous wood to breathe its bouquet on the salads. You may wish to reserve a separate garlic-free and onion-free bowl, just as some cooks do with cutting boards.

French cooks have given us the **chapon,** another method of instilling garlic's essence in tossed salads. Take a fairly dry piece of Italian or French bread, about an inch or two in thickness. Rub all sides of the bread generously with the cut garlic. Place the bread in the bowl with all the salad ingredients. Add the dressing and toss. Remove and discard the *chapon*.

MAKING YOUR OWN CROUTONS

Making croutons is one of the easiest things to do and a great "green kitchen" process—you get to recycle stale bread that you may otherwise have thrown out. Use any dry bread, white or whole grain. Slice the bread (with or without the crust, as desired) into about 1/2- to 1-inch size cubes. Allow about 1 tablespoon of butter or olive oil (or combination of both) per cup of bread cubes and about 1 teaspoon of dried herbs or 1 tablespoon of fresh herbs. Heat the oil or butter in a heavy skillet, add the bread cubes, and toss to coat well. Toast over moderate heat. Add the crumbled or chopped herbs. (Thyme by itself or in a mixture of other herbs makes for nicely seasoned croutons.) Toss the cubes occasionally so they brown as evenly as possible. Add a little salt and pepper if desired. Add warm to salad or allow to cool and store them in the refrigerator. Generally, add croutons after you've dressed the salad and toss again. Otherwise, croutons will become too soaked with dressing.

RECIPE NOTE

You will note that many of the recipes that follow in this book call for olive oil—either extra-virgin or just olive oil. Extra-virgin is specified when quality is important. Otherwise olive oil, which can mean pure olive oil, the cheapest grade, is fine to use. For more about olive oil grading see Salad Oils, page 107.

Arugula and Redleaf with Sautéed Mushrooms

Although you may be tempted to choose a richer dressing for this salad, it's not recommended. The pepperiness of the arugula and the sweet butter flavor and texture of the mushrooms should not be upstaged. For a special treat, try buttery-flavored chanterelles or other robust wild mushrooms.

Serves 4

½	**pound fresh mushrooms**
2	**tablespoons unsalted butter**
2	**tablespoons white wine vinegar**
½	**teaspoon Dijon mustard**
4	**tablespoons extra-virgin olive oil**
1	**head arugula, washed and torn into bite-size pieces**
1	**small head redleaf lettuce, washed and torn into bite-size pieces**
	Salt and pepper to taste

Wipe the mushrooms clean with a damp paper towel and slice them. Sauté the mushrooms in the butter over moderately high heat, stirring constantly for about 3 minutes. Remove from pan.

Combine the vinegar, mustard, and oil, and mix well. Toss dressing with the lettuces. Divide salad among 4 plates, topping each serving with some mushrooms. Season to taste.

Caesar Salad with Herbed Focaccia Croutons

The Caesar is a classic salad that has been around since the 1920s, when it was concocted by a chef in Tijuana, Mexico. If you can't find a loaf of herbed focaccia bread, use Italian or French bread and add your own herbs—some thyme and oregano. Use only the light-colored inner leaves of romaine and only the best Parmesan.

Serves 4

4	tablespoons ($\frac{1}{2}$ stick) butter
1	loaf herbed focaccia bread, cut into 1-inch cubes (about 3 cups)
2	cloves garlic, minced
1	egg
2	anchovy fillets, mashed
$\frac{1}{4}$	cup lemon juice
5	tablespoons olive oil
$\frac{1}{2}$	cup coarsely grated Parmesan cheese
2	large heads romaine, inner light leaves only
	Freshly ground black pepper, to taste
	Extra grated Parmesan for garnish

Melt the butter in a large skillet and add the bread cubes and garlic. Toast over moderate heat for about 5 minutes, stirring cubes often until golden on all sides. Remove from heat and set aside.

Boil egg for 1 minute, then break it into a bowl, scraping it from the shell with a spoon. Whisk in anchovies, lemon juice, olive oil, and Parmesan cheese, and blend until smooth.

Toss whole lettuce leaves with dressing, then arrange them on 4 salad plates. Sprinkle each salad with croutons and parmesan. Garnish with freshly ground black pepper.

Mediterranean Deli Salad

Serves 4

1	cucumber, peeled
1	green pepper, coarsely chopped
1	large firm, ripe tomato, sliced into wedges
$\frac{1}{2}$	red onion, thinly sliced
1	heart of iceberg lettuce, chopped
$\frac{1}{4}$	cup chopped flatleaf parsley
$\frac{1}{4}$	cup red wine vinegar
1	teaspoon crumbled, dried oregano
$\frac{1}{2}$	teaspoon salt
$\frac{1}{2}$	teaspoon black pepper
$\frac{1}{3}$	cup olive oil

Quarter the cucumber lengthwise. Slice each quarter into $\frac{1}{2}$-inch pieces. Toss the cucumber, pepper, tomato, onion, lettuce, and parsley together. Combine the vinegar, oregano, salt, pepper, and oil, and mix well. Toss dressing with salad and serve.

Vegetable Pinwheel Platter

This is another "crowd" salad—good for sit-down dinners or as part of a buffet.

Serves 6 to 8

1	small head spinach
1	head greenleaf lettuce
3–4	boiled red potatoes, sliced
2	hard-cooked eggs, sliced (optional)
1	cup olives, sliced
1	sweet red pepper, julienned
1	cup grated purple cabbage
1	carrot, grated
	Herbed French Dressing, 114, Blue Cheese Dressing, 119, or Lemon Poppyseed Dressing, 121, borage blossoms or johnny jump-ups (optional garnish)

Wash and dry the greens and keep them whole. Arrange them on a big tray platter. Arrange the potato and egg slices on the greens in concentric circles. Place olive slices on top of potatoes and egg. Sprinkle any remaining olives around greens.

Mound the julienned pepper and grated cabbage and carrot in three piles in the center of platter. Pour some dressing over center vegetables and a thin stream over potatoes and eggs. Scatter a few borage blossoms and/or johnny jump-ups around as garnish. Serve any remaining dressing separately in a small pitcher.

Mexican Salad

Serves 4 to 6

$\frac{1}{2}$ **cup jicama matchsticks**
1   **tablespoon lime juice**
$\frac{1}{2}$ **cup cooked corn, at room temperature**
$\frac{1}{4}$ **cup diced sweet red pepper**
$\frac{1}{4}$ **cup nopales (cactus pads)* or sliced, cooked green beans**
$\frac{1}{3}$ **cup sliced olives**
6–7   **cups mixed firm and soft greens, such as romaine, iceberg, redleaf, and butter lettuces**
$\frac{2}{3}$ **cup Mild Salsa Dressing, page 116, or Spicy Mexican Dressing, page 113**

Toss the jicama with the lime juice and set aside to marinate about 20 minutes.

Combine the corn, pepper, nopales, and olives and arrange on top of mixed greens in a large bowl or in individual servings. Add the jicama last. Serve with Mild Salsa Dressing or Spicy Mexican Dressing on the side or pass at the table.

*Available in Mexican foods section of supermarkets.

Braised Fennel with Sage

This is a great appetizer or side dish for a hearty Italian dinner, especially one including fish (fish and fennel attract). Also consider including Braised Fennel as part of an antipasto tray.

Serves 6 to 8 as an appetizer

3   **medium-size bulbs fennel**
3   **cups chicken stock**
1   **cup sweet Marsala**
2   **tablespoons chopped fresh sage**
12   **oil-preserved sun-dried tomatoes, coarsely chopped**
3   **tablespoons extra-virgin olive oil**
   Freshly ground black pepper
   Fresh sage leaves

Preheat oven to 350°F. Remove the tough green tops of the fennel and slice off the root end. Slice each bulb into 8 to 10 wedges. Place the fennel in a baking dish and add stock, Marsala, and sage. Bake until fennel is tender, about 45 minutes. With a slotted spoon, remove fennel and chill.

Sprinkle tomatoes and oil over fennel. Garnish with pepper and fresh sage leaves.

Rainbow Salad with Rémoulade

Serves 4 to 6

2	cups grated celery root
2	cups grated carrots
2	cups grated fresh beets
1	tablespoon drained capers
1	tablespoon white wine vinegar
2	tablespoons chopped sweet pickles
1	egg yolk
¼	cup olive oil
¼	cup peanut oil
1	teaspoon Dijon mustard
2	anchovy fillets, mashed
1	tablespoon minced fresh tarragon
⅛	teaspoon cayenne pepper

Parboil the grated celery root, carrots, and beets, separately, for 3 minutes each. Drain and set aside to cool.

Combine the capers, vinegar, and pickles in a small cup and set aside. Place the egg yolk in a medium-size bowl and beat with a wire whisk until lemon yellow. Slowly beat in the olive oil. Sauce will become very thick as it emulsifies. Alternately add the vinegar mixture and peanut oil slowly. If more liquid is needed, slowly add a tablespoon of warm water. Stir in remaining ingredients and mix well.

Arrange grated vegetables in three separate heaps on individual plates. Spoon sauce over vegetables or pass a pitcher of sauce at the table.

Variation: Arrange all vegetables on a large platter with a well in the center for a small bowl of the sauce.

Asparagus with Lemon Garlic Cream

This makes an elegant side dish to a fancy dinner.

Serves 4 to 6

1	pound fresh asparagus
½	cup Creamy Lemon Garlic Dressing, page 119
3	tablespoons heavy cream
	Freshly ground black pepper
3-4	threads or thin gratings of lemon zest*
	Fresh sprigs parsley or basil

Trim away any tough ends of the asparagus. Steam them just until bright green, about 3 minutes. Chill.

Combine Creamy Lemon Garlic dressing with heavy cream. Drizzle over chilled asparagus and garnish with black pepper, lemon zest, and fresh herb sprigs.

*A citrus zesting tool works best to achieve long thin "threads" of lemon peel. But you can also grate the lemon with the coarse section of a cheese grater.

Spinach Salad with Hot Bacon Dressing

Combining the earthiness of greens such as spinach with the robustness of salted ham or bacon, this salad has its origins in the South.

Serves 4

¼	pound (6 strips) bacon
⅓	cup cream sherry
1	tablespoon brown sugar
½	teaspoon salt
3	tablespoons olive or peanut oil
1	large head or 2 small heads fresh spinach, stemmed, washed and dried
2	hard-cooked eggs, sieved
	Black pepper

Fry the bacon until crisp. Remove to paper toweling to drain. Reserve renderings.

In a small saucepan heat the sherry, sugar, and salt until it starts to boil slightly. Allow to boil gently for 3 minutes, stirring. Over low heat, stir in 3 tablespoons reserved bacon drippings and oil. Cook just until heated through, about 3 minutes.

Crumble bacon. Toss spinach leaves with dressing and top with bacon and eggs. Serve immediately.

Red Onion and Cucumber Salad

Serves 4 to 6

¼   cup red wine vinegar
2   teaspoons sugar
1   large European cucumber, very thinly sliced
1   small red onion, sliced into paper-thin rings
     Salt and pepper to taste

In a bowl, combine vinegar and sugar. Toss in cucumber and onion and mix well. Chill. Add salt and pepper to taste just before serving.

Cucumber with Mint-Yogurt Salad

This goes well with roast lamb or with any Mid-Eastern fare.

Serves 4 to 6 as side dish

1   medium-size seedless cucumber
1   clove garlic
½   teaspoon salt
¼   teaspoon black pepper
¼   cup chopped fresh mint leaves
2¼ cups yogurt

Peel the cucumber and quarter it lengthwise. Slice into quarter-inch pieces.

Pound the garlic, salt, and pepper together in a mortar and pestle or purée in a blender. Stir garlic mixture and mint leaves into yogurt. Stir in cucumber. Serve immediately or chill.

Serving suggestion: If you can find juicy, ripe tomatoes, slice and arrange them on a platter. Pile the cucumber salad on top. Garnish with fresh mint.

Redleaf, Avocado, and Red Onion

Serves 6

1   medium-size head redleaf, washed
1   small head escarole, washed
1   cup Herbed French Dressing, page 114
1   firm, ripe avocado, peeled and sliced
1   small red onion, very thinly sliced and
      separated into rings
1   red pepper, cored and sliced into rings
1   yellow pepper, cored and sliced into rings
1   cup cherry tomatoes, washed and halved
½   cup radishes, sliced
1   carrot, peeled into ribbons

Toss the greens with the dressing. Add the avocado, onion rings, peppers, tomatoes, radishes, and carrot ribbons and toss again gently.

Warm Tomato Salad with Tapenade Dressing

This recipe will enliven a mediocre batch of tomatoes. Save your perfect tomatoes for the previous recipe. Slightly cooking the tomatoes coaxes forth their tomato-y essence.

Serves 4 as a side dish

2½–3   pounds firm, ripe tomatoes, sliced rather thickly

1   head butter lettuce, washed and broken into whole leaves

½   cup Tapenade Dressing, page 115
        Fresh basil, chervil, or parsley leaves (optional)

Heat the tomato slices in a nonstick pan, such as Silverstone, just until they start to sizzle and run juicy, but not until they fall apart. With a spatula, turn and cook the other side. Place 2 or 3 lettuce leaves on each salad plate and divide the tomatoes among them.

Spoon some dressing over each salad, and top with a sprig of fresh herb, if desired, and serve immediately.

Jicama, Fennel, and Red Pepper

This is a nice party appetizer.

Serves 4 to 6 as side dish

1	large bulb fennel, trimmed and cut into matchsticks
1	small jicama, peeled and cut into matchsticks
1	large sweet red pepper, cut into matchsticks
	Juice of 1 lemon
½	teaspoon sugar
½	teaspoon salt
	Freshly ground pepper
2	tablespoons extra-virgin olive oil

Toss the fennel, jicama, and red pepper together in a salad bowl. In a measuring cup, stir the lemon, sugar, salt, ground pepper to taste, and oil together and pour over the salad. Toss to coat well.

Cauliflower with Oriental Dressing

Serve this exotically seasoned salad with any dish with which you would serve cauliflower. It also goes well on a cold buffet.

Serves 4 to 6

1	medium-size head of cauliflower, broken into florets
3	tablespoons balsamic vinegar
4	tablespoons soy sauce
½	teaspoon five-spice powder*
½	teaspoon sugar
3	tablespoons olive oil
3	tablespoons peanut oil
1	teaspoon hot pepper oil (optional)
¼	cup minced sweet red pepper
3	tablespoons toasted pine nuts

Steam the cauliflower for 20 minutes, then place in refrigerator to cool for about 20 minutes. Combine vinegar, soy, five-spice powder, sugar, and oils. Toss cauliflower with dressing. Add pepper and pine nuts and serve.

*Available in Asian food markets or see recipe following:

Five-Spice Powder

2   **whole star anise***
1   **teaspoon fennel seeds**
1   **teaspoon black pepper**
½   **teaspoon ground cloves**
1   **teaspoon ground cinnamon**

     Grind or pound the star anise and fennel seeds together until a fine powder. Mix with remaining ingredients. Store in a jar.

*Available in Asian food markets.

Health Nut Salad

Serves 4

1   head Bibb lettuce, washed and cut into
    bite-size pieces
½   cup Tomato-Tamari Dressing, page 116
1   cup mixed sprouts (alfalfa, sunflower, radish,
    mung, lentil)*
¼   cup tamari-roasted whole almonds*
¼   cup dried currants and/or dried cranberries
3   tablespoons pepitas (pumpkin seeds)

First toss the lettuce with the dressing in a salad bowl. Arrange the sprouts on top. Toss the remaining ingredients together and sprinkle on top.

*Available at health food stores.

Roasted Pepper and Feta Appetizer

Serve this tasty appetizer with crusty Italian or peasant bread.

Serves 4 to 6 as appetizer

4   large sweet red peppers
⅓   cup extra-virgin olive oil
2   tablespoons balsamic vinegar
¼   teaspoon salt
    Freshly ground black pepper, to taste
4   ounces low-salt feta cheese, crumbled
2   tablespoons chopped fresh basil or Italian
    parsley, optional

Preheat broiler. Place peppers under broiler and cook, turning them often, until skins are very charred. You can also char pepper skins by holding each pepper at the end of a fork and turning it over an open flame. Place the peppers in a paper bag and place that inside a plastic bag (peppers may run and break through the paper). Place inside the refrigerator and allow peppers to sweat at least 30 minutes (you can leave them overnight). When cool enough to handle, remove skins, seeds, and stems. Do not rinse peppers. Place them whole or sliced into strips on a serving platter.

Combine oil, vinegar, salt, and pepper and drizzle over peppers. Sprinkle crumbled feta over peppers and garnish with chopped herbs, if desired.

Chilled Artichokes with *Bagna Cauda* and *Grissini*

Bagna cauda refers to the "warm bath," which serves as a tasty dip for raw or cooked vegetables. *Grissini,* Italian bread sticks, which can be found with or without sesame seeds, are traditionally served with this dip. Serve this as an appetizer to distract waiting dinner guests.

Serves 4

¼   **pound (1 stick) butter**
⅓   **cup olive oil**
1   **clove garlic**
¼   **teaspoon salt**
2   **anchovy fillets**
8   ***grissini***
4   **large steamed and chilled artichokes**

Melt the butter in a saucepan. Combine butter, oil, garlic, salt, and anchovies in a blender or food processor and process until smooth. Return mixture to saucepan and heat until very hot, but not boiling. Pour sauce into a bowl or two for dipping at the table. Serve 2 bread sticks with each artichoke.

Italian Appetizer Antipasto

This makes a good hors d'oeuvre for a crowd. Include it on a holiday buffet spread.

Serves 6 to 8 as an appetizer

1	medium-size head spinach or redleaf lettuce, or a combination of both
¾	pound buffalo milk or part-skim mozzarella, cut into ¼-inch slices
20–30	sun-dried tomatoes, rehydrated (preferably not marinated)
1	sweet red pepper
1	teaspoon dried, crumbled oregano Anchovy Dressing, page 116

Wash and dry the greens and keep them whole. Arrange them on a large tray or platter (about 15 inches in diameter) in rosette fashion. Distribute the mozzarella evenly in concentric circles. Place a sun-dried tomato on each slice of cheese.

Remove the stem and seeds from the pepper, keeping it whole. With a small sharp knife, slice the pepper around its girth into one or several long, thin spirals. Pile the strips in the center of the platter in rose fashion.

Stir the oregano into the Anchovy Dressing and sprinkle it over the antipasto.

Orange Beet Salad

Serves 4 to 6

2	pounds beets, washed and trimmed
½	yellow onion, thinly sliced
	Juice of 1 whole orange
1	teaspoon grated orange zest
¼	cup cider vinegar
½	cup corn oil
½	teaspoon salt
¼	cup chopped fresh parsley

In a large pot, cover the beets with water. Bring to a boil and simmer until tender, about 45 minutes. Drain beets, and when cool enough to handle, peel and slice into ½-inch wedges. Combine beets with onions.

Combine the orange juice and zest, vinegar, oil, and salt, and mix well. Pour dressing over beets and mix well. Chill and garnish with parsley before serving.

Orange-Braised Red Cabbage

This is a delicious holiday salad, great with game or fowl main dishes.

Serves 6 to 8 as a side dish

3½ – 4	pounds purple cabbage, shredded
1	quart orange juice
⅓	cup cider vinegar
2	tablespoons corn oil
1½	teaspoons caraway, optional
6 – 8	thin slices of orange

Combine cabbage and orange juice in a heavy-bottom skillet, cover, and bring to a boil. Cook over high heat for 10 minutes, then lower heat and simmer cabbage, uncovered, for 45 minutes or until very tender. Strain cabbage and reserve ¼ cup cooking liquid.

Combine cooking liquid with vinegar, oil, and caraway. Toss with cabbage. Garnish with orange slices and chill.

Variation: Add a dollop of sour cream or yogurt to each serving.

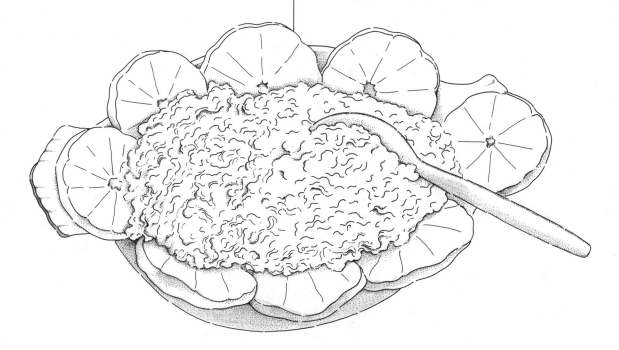

Vegetable Ribbons with Toasted Sesame Dressing

Serves 4 to 6 as side dish

2	**large carrots**
2	**medium-size zucchini**
2	**small crookneck squash**
½	**cup Toasted Sesame Dressing, page 115**

Peel carrots. Using a mandoline, vegetable parer, or similar device, slice carrots into wide ribbons. Use as much of the carrot as possible. Peel skin from one area of zucchini, then, starting there, pare into wide strips. (Zucchini is pretty with a thin strip of green skin on either side of ribbons.) Peel and pare crookneck squash in same manner as zucchini. Arrange ribbons on a platter and sprinkle with some Toasted Sesame Dressing. Serve remaining dressing in a small pitcher.

Japanese Pickled Vegetables (*Namasu*)

This is a refreshing starter or side dish for most Asian meals. It keeps well for a few weeks. If you don't have a food processor to quickly julienne all the vegetables, you can shred them with the coarse grating section of a cheese grater.

Serves 4 to 6 as side dish

2	tablespoons chopped pickled ginger*
½	cup brown rice vinegar*
2	tablespoons sugar
1	teaspoon salt
3	drops dark sesame oil
2	medium-size carrots, peeled and julienned
1	medium-size turnip, peeled and julienned
1	medium-size daikon, peeled and julienned**
½	seedless, unwaxed (European) cucumber*** (about 4½ inches), unpeeled and cut into matchsticks (or 1 medium-size cucumber, peeled and cut into matchsticks)

Place ginger, vinegar, sugar, salt, and sesame oil in a salad bowl and mix well. Toss in all vegetables and stir to coat well. Allow salad to marinate in refrigerator for 1 hour before serving.

*Available at Asian food stores.
**Daikon, an Oriental radish, is usually available in most produce markets, but most definitely in Chinese markets.
***The European, or English, cucumber is readily available in the produce section of most supermarkets. It's the longer, thinner one, sometimes wrapped tightly in cellophane or plastic.

Avocado with Shrimp and Fresh Oregano

This is a very simple but delicious appetizer, best when avocados are at their peak.

Serves 4

2	ripe but firm avocados
4	tablespoons balsamic vinegar
4	tablespoons extra-virgin olive oil
4	tablespoons cooked baby shrimp
4	teaspoons minced fresh oregano
	Freshly ground black pepper

Do not peel avocados. With a sharp knife, slice each one in half lengthwise and remove the pit with the point of the knife. Place each half on a platter and place one-fourth of the vinegar, oil, shrimp, and oregano in the hollow. Garnish with pepper.

Tomato Salad
(Insalata Pomodoro)

Make this only with the best tomatoes—ideally those just picked from your own garden. They must be plump, red, and fragrant with juice and pulp. Allow one tomato per person. If you can't get great tomatoes, try warm Tomato Salad with Tapenade Sauce, page 35.

Ripe tomatoes, sliced
Finest extra-virgin olive oil
Salt and fresh ground pepper
Oregano, fresh or dried

Fill a platter with slices of the tomatoes. Generously drizzle with the olive oil, preferably a thick, fruity, green one. Sprinkle with salt and pepper. Rub the oregano between the palms of your hands as you sprinkle it over the salad. Serve with crusty wedges of bread—your guests will leave no trace of dressing.

Marinated Mushrooms

The button or field mushroom has been overshadowed by the many wild varieties now available. Button mushrooms are still good hearty ones, great for marinades. This goes well on a buffet or as part of a cold antipasto.

1	**pound medium-size button mushrooms**
3	**tablespoons white wine vinegar**
2	**shallots, minced**
$\frac{1}{4}$	**teaspoon ground nutmeg**
$\frac{1}{2}$	**teaspoon salt**
$\frac{1}{2}$	**teaspoon black pepper**
1	**tablespoon minced fresh tarragon**
$\frac{1}{3}$	**cup olive oil**

Boil 2 quarts salted water and drop the mushrooms in. Drain after 3 minutes.

Combine the vinegar, shallots, nutmeg, salt, pepper, tarragon, and oil. Toss with the mushrooms to coat well. Marinate at least one hour.

Chapter Two

MAIN DISHES

The recipes in this section are based on cheese combined with meat, fish, chicken, or other poultry, and are hearty enough to take center stage in a menu. In some cases, just the addition of some good bread and maybe a light soup accompaniment completes the menu.

Meat, fish, and fowl are no longer unusual foundations for a salad. Indeed, other cultures, which have had much more experience at stretching meat and protein foods, have invented delicious salads with such ingredients for ages. Asian cookery lends wonderful new dimension to meats with its vast array of aromatic herbs and exotic spices. And American cooks have been very quick to adapt the best of these to our current taste in adventurous dining.

Just about any cut of meat, fowl, or fish can be worked into a salad. Such salads can be served as the main course of a dinner or lunch menu (you may find the recipe goes further for a lunch menu). Meat and fowl can be left over or freshly cooked. If left over, they should not be too far past their prime, as no amount of doctoring can restore freshness.

For fish salads, only the freshest catch will do. And it can be cooked in the simplest manner. Poaching and grilling are generally good cooking methods for fish to be served in salad. Remember the acid of the marinade that may form the dressing actually cooks the flesh (as in the well-known ceviche). For this reason, I recommend undercooking the fish to retain some moisture, which also enhances flavor. Usually firm-fleshed fish, such as most shellfish, tuna, swordfish, salmon, and halibut, are best suited for salad treatment. Delicate-fleshed fish such as sole and whiting tend to fall apart in salad and their fragile flavors are perhaps done an injustice with most dressings.

GENERAL TIPS FOR MEAT AND FISH SALADS:

• Remove all fat and gristle. Cut meat across the grain into even-thickness strips. Arrange slices in a neat, decorative pattern on a platter.

• If using leftover meat that has been poached, use a sharp-flavored vinaigrette dressing to add back some moisture, robustness, and depth of flavor.

• Unless specified to be served warm or hot, most meat and fish salads taste best served at room temperature or just slightly chilled.

Sesame-Soy Shrimp with Napa Cabbage

Serves 4 to 6

1	**pound shrimp**
½	**cup soy sauce**
1	**clove garlic, mashed**
	Juice of 1 whole lemon
⅛	**teaspoon crushed red pepper or 1 small red chili, minced**
⅓	**cup peanut oil**
3	**tablespoons dark sesame oil**
1	**medium-size head napa cabbage,* cleaned and chopped into bite-size pieces**
2	**tablespoons chopped fresh cilantro**

Drop shrimp into salted boiling water, cover, and remove from heat. Allow to sit 10 minutes. Drain and, when cool enough to handle, shell and devein shrimp.

In a bowl, combine soy, garlic, lemon juice, pepper, and oils, and stir well. Add shrimp and toss to coat well. Marinate shrimp in dressing a few hours, tossing occasionally.

Toss cabbage in a serving bowl with enough marinade dressing to coat well. Arrange shrimp on top of cabbage. Garnish with cilantro.

*Napa (or Chinese) cabbage is fairly easy to find in most supermarket produce sections. If you can't find it, use a firm lettuce, such as iceberg or romaine, as a substitute.

Lamb, Mint, and Yogurt Salad

This Greek combination makes a great luncheon dish and is a good way to use your leftover Easter lamb.

Serves 4 to 6

1	clove garlic
$1/2$	teaspoon salt
1	cup plain yogurt
$1/2$	cup chopped fresh mint
4	cups diced cooked leg of lamb
$1/3$	cup toasted pine nuts
	Freshly ground black pepper, to taste

Mash garlic with salt and combine with yogurt and mint. Toss with lamb and pine nuts. Season with pepper to taste.

Grilled London Broil on Baby Lettuce

Serves 4

$1/2$	cup red wine vinegar
$1/2$	cup olive oil
1	teaspoon salt
1	teaspoon black pepper
1	tablespoon dried oregano
1	pound London broil
4	cups mixed baby lettuces
	Extra-virgin olive oil

Combine the vinegar, $1/2$ cup olive oil, salt, pepper, and oregano in a bowl with the meat. Marinate the meat for at least 1 hour, turning occasionally. Grill the meat to taste, using the marinade to baste. Slice the cooked meat on the bias into thin strips. Arrange the strips in circles on beds of the lettuce on 4 plates. Sprinkle a few drops of extra-virgin olive oil on each serving.

Pork and Shrimp Thai Salad

Serves 4 to 6

1	tablespoon minced garlic
2	tablespoons peanut oil
1	small head green cabbage, coarsely grated
2	small zucchini, coarsely grated
	Juice of 2 limes
3	tablespoons Thai fish sauce*
1	tablespoon palm sugar* (or brown sugar)
1	small red chili, thinly sliced (optional)
½	teaspoon salt
1	cup cooked pork
½	pound cooked shelled shrimp
2	tablespoons toasted coconut
2	tablespoons chopped roasted peanuts
1	tablespoon minced fresh cilantro

Sauté the garlic in the oil until golden, drain, and set aside.

Blanch the cabbage and zucchini together in boiling water for 1½ minutes. Drain and set aside to cool.

In a salad bowl, mix together lime juice, fish sauce, sugar, chili, and salt. Toss with cooled vegetables, pork, and shrimp. Sprinkle browned garlic, coconut, peanuts, and cilantro over top just before serving.

*Available in Asian food stores or markets.

Potato and Smoked Salmon Salad with Mustard Dressing

You can leave out the smoked salmon and still have a superb combination of flavors.

Serves 6 to 8

2½   dozen (about 1½ pounds) small new potatoes
¼   cup whole grain mustard
2   tablespoons Dijon or good French mustard
¼   cup white wine vinegar
2   tablespoons honey
½   teaspoon salt
½   teaspoon black pepper
½   cup plus 2 tablespoons peanut oil
½   cup chopped fresh dill
½   pound smoked salmon, cut into small pieces

Simmer the potatoes until tender, about 20 minutes. Drain and when cool enough to handle, cut into quarters.

Combine the mustards, vinegar, honey, salt, and pepper in a large salad bowl and mix well. Continue to mix with a wire whisk as you slowly drizzle in the oil. Beat constantly until smooth and blended. Stir in the dill. Toss in the potatoes and salmon and mix to coat well.

Cobb Salad

Cobb Salad was invented by Bob Cobb in the 1930s at the Brown Derby Restaurant in Hollywood. It was his rather elaborate version of a chef's salad.

Serves 6

½   cup olive oil
3   tablespoons white wine vinegar
2   tablespoons chopped fresh chives
½   teaspoon black pepper
4   cups chopped iceberg lettuce
2   cups chopped romaine lettuce
2   cups finely chopped cooked chicken or turkey breast
6   ounces bacon, cooked, drained, and crumbled
3   hard-cooked eggs, peeled and chopped
⅓   cup crumbled blue cheese
1   small or ½ medium-size firm-ripe avocado, peeled and diced
1   large tomato chopped

Mix the olive oil, vinegar, chives, and black pepper in the bottom of a salad bowl. Add the lettuces and toss to coat well.

Arrange the dressed lettuce on a large serving platter. Arrange the chicken or turkey, bacon, eggs, blue cheese, avocado, and tomato on top of the lettuce, in separate piles like spokes of a wheel. Pass the platter as is to each diner, or toss all together at the table and then serve.

Baked Chicken Salad with Tarragon-Lime Dressing

This makes a good entrée. Serve with some nice bread.

Serves 4 to 6

For the chicken:

1¼	pounds skinned, boned chicken breast
3	cloves garlic, minced
½	teaspoon salt
½	teaspoon black pepper
	Juice of 1 whole lime
3	tablespoons olive oil
2	tablespoons chopped fresh tarragon

For the dressing:

1	clove garlic
2	tablespoons chopped fresh tarragon
½	teaspoon salt
1	egg yolk
¼	cup olive oil
	Juice of 1 lime
⅓	cup peanut oil
4–6	cups mixed greens, such as frisée, arugula, radicchio, chicory, redleaf, or butter
	Freshly ground black pepper

Prepare chicken: Preheat oven to 350°F. Place chicken in a baking dish and rub with garlic, salt, pepper, lime juice, oil, and tarragon. Cover and bake for 30 minutes or until cooked through. Allow to cool enough to handle. Cut into 1-inch pieces.

Prepare dressing: Pound or puree garlic, 1 tablespoon tarragon, and salt to a paste. Set aside. Beat egg yolk with a wire whisk, and slowly whisk in olive oil. Whisk in a teaspoon lime juice to thin slightly and then alternately add lime juice with remaining oils until smooth and evenly mixed. Stir in tarragon mixture and remaining tarragon.

Spread greens on a large platter and arrange chicken on top. Drizzle dressing over chicken pieces and greens. Garnish salad with freshly ground black pepper.

Smoked Turkey Salad with Cranberries, Toasted Walnuts, and Goat Cheese Dressing

You can use Thanksgiving's leftover turkey in place of the smoked turkey here. Serve as a luncheon or dinner salad.

Serves 4 to 6

¼	**cup Grand Marnier**
2	**tablespoons sherry vinegar**
1	**tablespoon sugar**
¾	**cup fresh cranberries**
¼	**cup goat cheese**
⅓	**cup milk**
¼	**cup sour cream**
1	**tablespoon fresh lemon juice**
4	**cups boned, skinned, julienned smoked turkey**
½	**cup oven-toasted walnut halves**
	Freshly ground pepper
	Watercress sprigs

In a skillet, combine Grand Marnier, vinegar, and sugar and cook until sugar is dissolved and mixture is slightly reduced, about 7 minutes. Stir in cranberries and cook about 5 minutes, or until their skins split. Strain cranberries and set aside.

Whisk together the goat cheese, milk, sour cream, and lemon juice until smoothly blended.

Toss the turkey, cranberries, and walnut halves with the dressing. Garnish each serving with freshly ground pepper and watercress sprigs.

Serving Suggestion: Serve the salad in upturned leaves of radicchio—edible ramekins.

Sautéed Chicken on Mixed Greens with Creamy Pesto

Serves 4

3   tablespoons unsalted butter
3   tablespoons olive oil
2   cloves garlic, minced
2¹/₂   pounds chicken, cut into serving pieces
        Salt and pepper
6   cups mixed greens (baby chicory, mizuna,
        arugula, red- and greenleaf lettuces)
³/₄   cup Creamy Pesto Dressing, page 122

Preheat oven to 350°F.

Combine butter, oil, and garlic in a heavy ovenproof skillet. Add chicken parts and sauté until golden brown on all sides, about 7 minutes. Season to taste with salt and pepper. Transfer to oven and bake just until cooked through, about 30 minutes. Allow to cool slightly.

Arrange cooked chicken on 4 beds of mixed greens and drizzle dressing over each serving.

Variation: This recipe works very well with rabbit, quail, pheasant, or other game birds in place of the chicken.

Roasted Chicken with Young Spinach

You can, if you prefer, grill the chicken instead of roasting.

Serves 4

8   chicken parts (such as thighs, drumsticks, or
        breast halves)
2   cloves garlic, halved
        Lemon juice
        Olive oil
        Salt and pepper
4   tablespoons butter
¹/₄   cup olive oil
2   tablespoons champagne or white wine vinegar
6   cups young spinach leaves

Preheat oven to 375°F.

Rub the chicken pieces liberally with garlic, lemon juice, and olive oil, then sprinkle with salt and pepper. In a heavy skillet, sauté chicken in butter until lightly brown, about 7 minutes.

Transfer chicken to roasting pan and place in oven. Roast for 20 to 30 minutes, just until juices begin to run clear.

Combine ¹/₄ cup olive oil and vinegar and toss with spinach leaves. Arrange 2 pieces of chicken for each serving on bed of dressed spinach leaves.

Note: For a more exotic recipe, try roasted quail or duck in place of the chicken.

Avocado-Chicken Salad

For an eye-catching presentation, serve this salad in hollowed-out tomatoes or red, green, or yellow bell peppers—slice off the bottom of the peppers so they'll stand upright. This also makes a good sandwich spread.

Serves 4 to 6

4	**cups diced, cooked chicken**
1	**medium-ripe avocado, peeled and coarsely mashed**
2	**stalks celery, finely chopped**
1	**small green pepper, finely chopped**
¼	**cup minced onion**
1	**hard-cooked egg, chopped**
¾	**cup mayonnaise**
2	**teaspoons mustard**
½	**teaspoon salt**
½	**teaspoon black pepper**
1	**head green- or redleaf lettuce, washed and torn into whole leaves**
6	**tablespoons chopped fresh parsley**

Combine all ingredients, except parsley and lettuce, and mix well. Arrange lettuce leaves on large platter or on individual serving plates and mound salad on top. Garnish with chopped fresh parsley.

Smoked Duck with Apples, Walnuts, and Endive

Serves 4

1	3-pound smoked duck*
1	tablespoon lemon juice
1	tablespoon champagne vinegar
1	tablespoon honey
1	teaspoon Dijon mustard
$\frac{1}{2}$	teaspoon salt
$\frac{1}{2}$	teaspoon black pepper
2	teaspoons minced fresh herbs (such as parsley, basil, tarragon, chervil, and thyme)
$\frac{1}{4}$	cup walnut oil
$\frac{1}{4}$	cup olive or other vegetable oil
2	heads Belgian endive
1	tart green apple, cored and chopped, not peeled
$\frac{1}{2}$	cup toasted walnut halves

Remove the duck's skin and bones and slice the meat into julienne strips.

Whisk together the lemon juice, vinegar, honey, mustard, salt, pepper, and herbs. In a stream, whisk in the walnut and olive oils.

Remove the outer endive leaves. Slice the remaining endive and toss with the duck, apple, walnuts, and dressing.

*Available in Asian markets and specialty food shops.

Grilled Salmon, Watercress, and Orange Salad

Serves 4

1	pound salmon fillet
	Lemon juice
	Olive oil
2	medium-size oranges
2	tablespoons lemon juice
$\frac{1}{4}$	cup extra-virgin olive oil
4	tablespoons chopped fresh parsley
$\frac{1}{2}$	teaspoon salt
$\frac{1}{2}$	teaspoon black pepper
1	bunch watercress
$\frac{1}{4}$	cup toasted sliced almonds

Cut the salmon into 1-inch-wide strips. Rub the strips with the basting lemon juice and olive oil and grill. Do not overcook.

Peel the oranges and remove all the membrane from each section. If the membrane is too stubborn to remove with your hands, use a sharp knife and, working over a bowl to catch the juice, slice the orange pulp away from the membrane. Set the orange sections aside.

Combine the collected orange juice with the 2 tablespoons lemon juice, extra-virgin olive oil, parsley, salt, and pepper. Toss the watercress and orange sections with the dressing. Arrange the salad on 4 plates. Top each plate with slices of cooked salmon and almonds.

Fresh Tuna with
Hot Pepper–Lime Dressing

You can make this recipe a day ahead, adding the onions and cilantro just before serving, if desired. You can substitute monkfish for the tuna.

Serves 4 to 6

1	**small chili, thinly sliced**
¼	**cup olive oil**
2	**tablespoons peanut oil**
1	**carrot**
1	**rib of celery**
3	**sprigs parsley**
1	**teaspoon anise seeds**
1½	**teaspoons salt**
½	**teaspoon black peppercorns**
1	**cup white wine**
1½	**pounds fresh tuna steak**
	Juice of 2 whole limes
½	**teaspoon black pepper**
3	**thin slices red onion, separated into rings**
2	**tablespoons chopped fresh cilantro or Italian parsley**

Combine sliced chili with olive oil and peanut oil and set aside for an hour or longer to infuse.

In a large pot, combine carrot, celery, parsley, anise, 1 teaspoon salt, and peppercorns with 2 quarts water. Bring to a boil and allow to cook for 30 minutes. Add wine and cook another 20 minutes. Turn down to a simmer, add tuna, and cook about 5 minutes or just until tuna is opaque on the outside, but still pink on the inside when tested with a fork. Remove tuna and set aside to cool slightly.

Strain chili from oil, if desired, or leave in for more piquancy. In a shallow bowl, combine oil, lime juice, remaining ½ teaspoon salt, and black pepper. Slice cooled tuna into bite-size pieces and toss with dressing. Distribute onion slices over tuna. Sprinkle cilantro or parsley on top (if reserving salad, do not add these until an hour before serving). Allow fish to marinate for about an hour at room temperature, tossing occasionally. If marinating longer, refrigerate.

Crab-Stuffed Tomatoes

Serves 4

8–12 small (about 2 inches diameter) firm, ripe
      tomatoes
2   cups cooked crab meat
3   tablespoons minced green pepper
1   tablespoon minced onion
½   cup mayonnaise
2   teaspoons Dijon mustard
1   tablespoon lemon juice
2   tablespoons chopped fresh parsley
2   tablespoons chopped fresh chives
½   teaspoon salt
8   lettuce leaves
12   thin cucumber slices
      Paprika

Using a small sharp knife, slice off the tops of the tomatoes. Carefully cut out the insides of each tomato. Use a spoon to scoop clean. Set tomato cups upside down to drain.

Combine remaining ingredients, except for cucumber, and mix well. Spoon crab mixture into tomato cups and pack down well. Place two lettuce leaves on each plate with two tomatoes on top. Garnish each with 3 cucumber slices and a sprinkling of paprika.

Warm Goat Cheese Salad

Serves 4

¼	cup walnut oil
2	tablespoons white wine vinegar
6	cups mixed salad greens (butter, romaine, loose-leaf)
8	ounces goat cheese, cut into 4 equal-size pieces
½	cup toasted walnut halves
	Fresh ground black pepper

Combine oil and vinegar and toss with lettuce. Arrange on 4 salad plates.

Place goat cheese on an oiled pan and broil about 4 inches below heat until cheese begins to toast slightly, about 5 minutes. Place 1 knob of cheese on each salad, garnish with walnut halves and generous amounts of black pepper.

Scallop and Shrimp Salad

Serves 4 to 6

¼	cup white wine vinegar
1	clove garlic, crushed
1	teaspoon whole-grain mustard
2	teaspoons drained capers
1	tablespoon chopped fresh tarragon or chervil
¼	teaspoon crushed red pepper
⅔	cup olive oil
½	pound cooked and shelled medium-size shrimp
½	pound cooked large scallops
3	tablespoons minced sweet red pepper
1	stalk celery, minced
8–10	lettuce leaves
⅓	cup Italian olives

In a salad bowl, combine vinegar, garlic, mustard, capers, tarragon, crushed red pepper, and olive oil. Toss in shrimp, scallops, sweet pepper, and celery, and mix well. Serve on a bed of lettuce, garnished with olives.

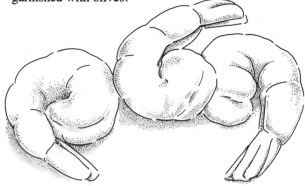

Chicken Breast and Sweet Basil in Roasted Pepper Sauce

Serves 4 to 6

For the chicken:

1½	**pounds skinned, boned chicken breast**
	Olive oil
	Lemon juice
	Salt and pepper

For the sauce:

4	**medium-size sweet red peppers**
3	**tablespoons red wine vinegar**
⅓	**cup extra-virgin olive oil**
½	**teaspoon salt**
½	**teaspoon black pepper**
8–10	**whole basil leaves**

Prepare the chicken: Preheat oven to 350°F. Rub the chicken with olive oil, then place it in a baking dish. Sprinkle with lemon juice, salt and pepper. Cover and bake 25 minutes or until done. Allow to cool.

Prepare the sauce: Roast peppers according to directions for Roasted Pepper and Feta Appetizer, page 38.

Puree the roasted peppers until very smooth. Measure out ½ cup pepper puree, reserving the rest to make more dressing (you can freeze it). Stir in the vinegar, oil, salt, and pepper.

Prepare the salad: Slice the cooled chicken into uniform strips. Pour the sauce on a large serving platter and distribute it evenly. Place the chicken strips on the sauce, pinwheel fashion. Distribute the basil leaves evenly in a rosette around the chicken. You can also arrange this salad in smaller serving portions.

Marinated Shrimp with Endive Boats

1	pound medium-size shrimp
1	small green pepper, minced
1	shallot, minced
1/4	cup white wine vinegar
1/2	teaspoon sugar
1/2	teaspoon salt
1/2	teaspoon black pepper
1/3	cup olive oil
2	tablespoons chopped Italian parsley
1	medium-size head of endive

Place the shrimp in salted boiling water, cover, and remove from heat. Let sit 10 minutes, drain, peel, and devein. Set aside to cool.

Combine all the remaining ingredients, except for endive, in a salad bowl and mix well. Add the shrimp and mix well. Chill and marinate shrimp several hours or overnight.

Arrange endive leaves like wheel spokes on a platter or tray. Fill each leaf with shrimp. Pile any extra salad in middle.

Cannelini and Sicilian Sausage

Serve this hearty salad warm or chilled.

Serves 6 to 8 as side dish or 4 to 6 as main dish (yields about 2 quarts)

2	cups cannelini (white) beans
1	carrot
1	rib celery
1	whole onion
1	bay leaf
3	sprigs parsley
1	teaspoon salt
1¼	pounds Sicilian sausage (fennel type)

Dressing:

⅓	cup white wine vinegar
	Juice of ½ lemon
⅓	cup olive oil
2	teaspoons black pepper
½	teaspoon salt
½	teaspoon crushed fennel seed
¼	cup chopped Italian parsley

Soak the beans overnight in cold water. In a 4-quart pot, cook beans with carrot, celery, onion, bay leaf, parsley, and salt for about 1 hour, until tender, but not mushy. Drain and allow to cool.

Meanwhile, cut sausage into 1-inch pieces and cook. Set aside to cool and drain on paper towel.

Make the dressing: In a large salad bowl, combine all the dressing ingredients and mix well. Stir in the cooled beans and sausage. Serve immediately or chill.

Variations: use 2–3 tablespoons fresh thyme instead of fennel in dressing. Add some chopped sun-dried tomatoes for color.

Salade Niçoise with Grilled Tuna

The *Salade Niçoise* originated in Provence, the sunny province in the south of France, where an abundance of seafood from the nearby Mediterreanean has long been used in many creative ways. The salad is usually made with canned tuna.

Serves 4

For the tuna:

1	pound fresh tuna steak
	Juice of 1 whole lemon
4	tablespoons olive oil

For the salad and dressing:

2	tablespoons white wine vinegar
1	teaspoon Dijon mustard
$\frac{1}{2}$	teaspoon salt
$\frac{1}{2}$	teaspoon black pepper
$\frac{1}{2}$	cup extra-virgin olive oil
2	medium-size tomatoes, cut into small wedges
2	cups cooked green beans, cut diagonally into 2-inch pieces
$\frac{1}{2}$	cup dry-cured olives
3	scallions, chopped
1	head butter lettuce, washed and torn into bite-size pieces
8	flat anchovies, drained
2	hard-cooked eggs, quartered
	Fresh sprigs parsley

Prepare the tuna: Brush the tuna with lemon juice and olive oil, and grill it on an oiled rack set about 4 inches above hot coals for 4 to 5 minutes on each side for medium-rare, or grill to taste. When cool enough to handle, cut into thin strips.

Prepare dressing and salad: In a salad bowl, combine vinegar, mustard, salt, pepper, and olive oil, and mix well. Add the tomatoes, beans, olives, scallions, and lettuce, and toss to coat with dressing. Add tuna and toss again. Garnish with anchovies, eggs, and parsley.

Note: If you can't grill the tuna, you can broil it instead.

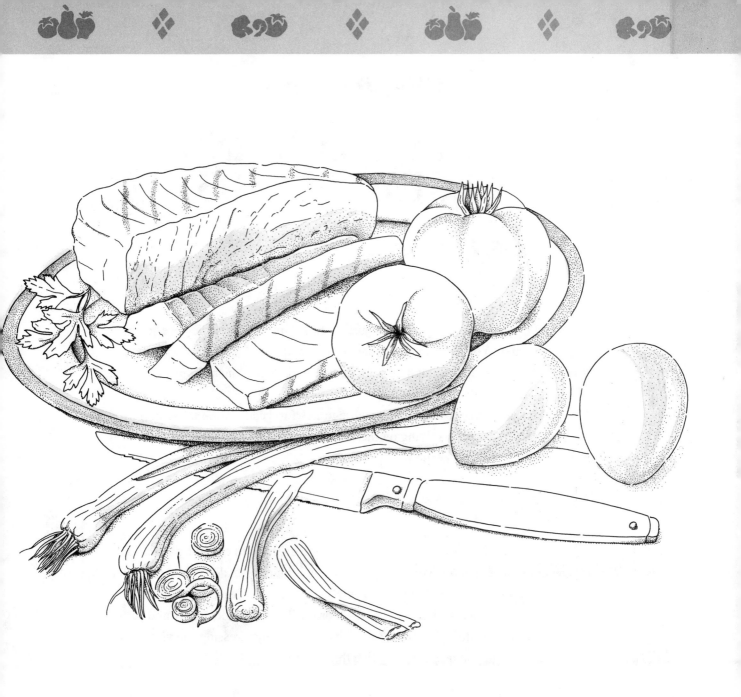

Chapter Three

PASTA, GRAIN, AND LEGUME SALADS

Pasta, grains, and legumes are just as filling in salads as they are in other types of dishes. You may find that some of the recipes in this section are interesting and filling enough to stand as main dish selections for lunch, brunch, or light dinner menus.

When you cook pasta, grains, and legumes for salads, cook them in lightly salted water, rather than relying on the dressing to add all the saltiness desired. It makes a difference in the end result.

PASTA

For pasta salads, make sure you add enough dressing to coat the pasta and all ingredients and that it is savory enough, as pasta is bland. But do not add too much dressing, or the pasta's own subtleties will be submerged. Cook the pasta *al dente* (slightly undercooked)—do not overcook it or it will become too mushy and soften under a vinaigrette dressing. If the salad sits too long, the dressing can also soften the pasta, though you may find you like this texture.

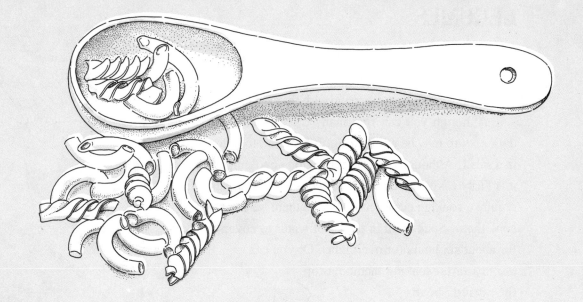

TIPS FOR PASTA SALADS:

• Use the firm store-bought pasta, not the softer hand-rolled or homemade pasta, which are too delicate for most salads.

• Of course pasta includes Asian noodles, too, such as soba (buckwheat), udon, and bewn thread, all of which make fine additions to salads. Check the instructions for cooking on each package, as they may vary.

• Do not rinse cooked pasta.

• Use sharp, aromatic, flavorful dressings, such as mustard-, garlic-, or cheese-embellished vinaigrettes.

• Add the dressing while the pasta is still warm, though pasta salads are best at room temperature or slightly chilled.

LEGUMES

Legumes includes peas, lentils, and a wide variety of dried beans. Their tastes and textures can vary quite a bit—even more so than with grains. Like grains, they are high in fiber and carbohydrates, and even higher in protein.

Although you can find many dried beans canned or frozen, their texture may be a little too soft for them to hold up well in a salad. Although beans require a long cooking period, it is fairly easy, low-maintenance cooking. Dried beans require a soaking period to rehydrate them before you cook them. Soak them in plenty of water to cover, for about six hours (or overnight). Or you can use this faster soaking method: drop the dried beans slowly into boiling water, let them boil about three minutes, then remove from the heat, and let the beans soak for one hour before cooking them. The pressure cooker is a great way to greatly reduce the cooking time of beans.

Again, salt beans during the cooking period. You can also add flavoring ingredients to the cooking water, such as a stalk of celery, a carrot, a bunch of parsley, garlic cloves, onion, spices, or a bouquet garni. In other words, anything aromatic will only enhance the flavor. Do not add oil or other fats, or acids such as vinegar or lemon juice, which may interfere with the cooking time.

Be careful not to overcook the beans. Most dried beans require from 45 to 75 minutes' cooking time (consult a cooking chart in any general cookbook) and generally do not easily overcook. Test the beans. They are done well enough for a salad when they are tender to the bite, but the seed coat is still fairly intact.

Unlike pasta and grains, bean salads will generally not become soggy and usually improve as they marinate in their dressing.

You can substitute any bean you like for most of the recipes given here. Experiment to find the combinations you like best.

GRAINS

Most cooked grains will work in a salad. Like pasta, they are mild-flavored ingredients and require enlivening from the dressing and the addition of other ingredients.

Cook the grain for salad to dry separateness, not mushy cohesiveness. Long or medium kernels of rice cook up the driest. Just a slight undercooking can keep them to dry and separate kernels. Use a little less water than called for. Grains usually require about 2 to 4 times their volume in cooking water.

Pasta and Shrimp with Sweet Balsamic Vinaigrette

Serves 4

4	ounces pancetta (Italian bacon)
½	pound rotelle, shells, or twists, cooked and drained
¾	pound shelled, deveined cooked shrimp
3	tablespoons chopped Italian parsley
½	cup Sweet Balsamic Vinaigrette, page 112

Chop the pancetta into small pieces, and sauté until crisp. Drain on paper towel, then toss with all remaining ingredients. Serve chilled or at room temperature.

Oriental Bean Thread and Tofu

The cellophane noodles cook quickly and absorb the dressing readily. This stores well for a few days.

Serves 4 to 6 as side dish

¼	cup soy sauce
2	tablespoons rice vinegar
2	teaspoons sesame oil
1	tablespoon minced fresh ginger
2	cloves garlic, mashed
10	ounces firm fresh tofu, cut into ½-inch cubes
6	ounces bean thread or cellophane noodles
2	small scallions, thinly sliced
2	carrots, julienned
2	stalks celery, julienned
10	baby corns, cut in half
1	sweet red pepper, julienned

Combine soy, vinegar, oil, ginger, and garlic and toss with tofu. Marinate tofu for at least one hour.

Drop bean thread into boiling water, remove from heat, and allow to soften for 20 minutes. Drain and allow to cool for a few minutes. Toss with marinated tofu (including marinade), taking care not to break tofu. Toss in remaining vegetables and mix well. Chill for 1 hour before serving.

Sicilian Salad
(*Insalata Siciliana*)

The fresh garlic used here is quite nice, but regular garlic is a fine substitute. Add the dressing while the shells are still hot from cooking.

Serves 6 to 8

$\frac{1}{3}$	cup red wine vinegar
$\frac{1}{4}$	cup finely grated imported Parmesan cheese
1	tablespoon fresh thyme
2	tablespoons chopped fresh (green) garlic or 1 teaspoon minced garlic
$\frac{1}{2}$	teaspoon salt
$\frac{3}{4}$	cup extra-virgin olive oil
1	pound pasta shells, cooked in salted water and drained
2	plum tomatoes, peeled, seeded, and chopped
$\frac{2}{3}$	cups Sicilian dry-cured olives
1	small green pepper, cut into thin 2-inch-long strips
$\frac{3}{4}$	cup rehydrated sun-dried tomatoes, chopped
6–8	ounces dried ricotta or low-salt feta, cut into $\frac{1}{2}$-inch cubes
$\frac{1}{2}$	cup chopped fresh parsley

Combine the vinegar, Parmesan, thyme, garlic, and salt, and stir well. Stir in the oil and mix well again. Combine remaining ingredients in a large bowl and toss with the dressing. Serve immediately or chill.

Tortellini with Vegetables and Garlic Vinaigrette

Using a mix of tortellini made from tomato, spinach, and egg makes this dish even more eye appealing.

Serves 4

2	tablespoons white wine vinegar
2	tablespoons lemon juice
1	tablespoon Dijon mustard
2	cloves garlic
$\frac{1}{2}$	teaspoon salt
$\frac{1}{2}$	teaspoon black pepper
$\frac{1}{2}$	cup extra-virgin olive oil
$\frac{1}{2}$	pound cooked cheese- or meat-stuffed tortellini
$1\frac{1}{2}$	cups steamed broccoli florets
1	cup steamed snow peas
1	sweet red pepper, chopped
$\frac{1}{2}$	cup pine nuts

Combine the vinegar, lemon juice, mustard, garlic, salt, pepper, and olive oil in a blender and process until smooth.

Mix the remaining ingredients in a salad bowl and toss with the dressing to mix well. Serve chilled or at room temperature.

Soba with Shiitake Mushrooms, Scallions, and Hot Sesame Soy Dressing

This Oriental salad is traditionally made with shiitake mushrooms, which you can find fresh or dried in Asian food markets. Regular button mushrooms may be substituted for the shiitake.

Serves 4 to 6

½	**cup peanut oil**
2	**tablespoons sesame oil**
1	**small hot red pepper, seeded and thinly sliced**
¼	**pound fresh shiitake mushrooms**
2	**tablespoons olive oil**
¼	**cup soy sauce**
2	**tablespoons rice (or cider) vinegar**
4	**scallions, thinly sliced**
1	**small sweet red pepper, julienned**
1	**pound soba noodles, cooked *al dente* and drained***

Combine peanut and sesame oils with sliced hot pepper and set aside to infuse overnight. Remove pepper from oil or leave in if you prefer a more fiery dressing.

Wipe any grit from the mushrooms with a damp paper towel. Remove and discard tough parts of stems. Slice caps thinly. Heat olive oil and sauté mushrooms over moderate heat for about 5 minutes. Set aside.

Combine peanut and sesame oil mixture with soy sauce and vinegar and toss with scallions, sweet red pepper, mushrooms, and noodles.

*Available in Asian food markets.

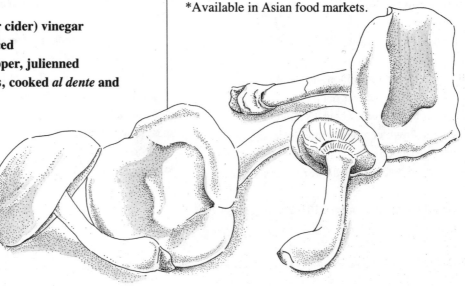

Cracked Wheat with Mint, Tomatoes, and Hazelnuts

The smallest tomatoes are best for this salad. Makes a great brunch or luncheon dish or side dish to lamb or game.

4	cups water
1½	teaspoons salt
2	cups cracked wheat (bulgur)
¼	cup fresh lemon juice
½	cup olive oil
½	cup chopped fresh mint leaves
1	teaspoon black pepper
3	scallions, thinly sliced
3	cups small red and yellow cherry or pear tomatoes
½	cup toasted hazelnuts

Boil water with 1 teaspoon salt. Add wheat, remove from heat, and cover pot tightly. Allow to sit until all water is absorbed, about 25 minutes.

In a large bowl, combine lemon juice, oil, remaining ½ teaspoon salt, mint, pepper and scallions. Mix well. Stir in cracked wheat. Stir in tomatoes and nuts.

Variation: Instead of nuts add 1½ cups chopped cooked chicken.

Wild Rice Salad with Apples and Toasted Pecans

Serves 6

1½	cups wild rice
3	cups rich chicken, meat, or vegetable stock
3	tablespoons olive oil
½	cup thinly sliced scallions
½	cup finely chopped celery
1	large red apple, not peeled, cored and diced
8	dried apricots or peaches, thinly sliced
¼	cup chopped parsley
2	tablespoons chopped fresh sage
	Salt and pepper to taste
	Bed of green leaf lettuce
1	cup pecan halves, toasted

Cook rice in stock until tender. Place rice in a bowl and set aside to cool about 20 to 30 minutes.

Heat the oil. Sauté the scallions, celery, and apple for 5 minutes. Stir in apricots or peaches, parsley, and sage, and adjust seasoning. Combine vegetable-fruit mixture with rice and toss to mix well.

Mound rice mixture on the bed of greens and compact slightly. Arrange pecan halves around the perimeter of rice mound.

Rice Salad with Grilled Radicchio and White Eggplant

If you can't find the sweeter white eggplant, use the purple.

Serves 6

1	cup long-grain rice
2	cups stock
1	medium-size white eggplant
½	cup olive oil
1	medium-size head radicchio
1	sweet red pepper, cut into thin strips
½	pound dried ricotta (or mozzarella), cut into ½-inch cubes
	Juice of 1 whole lemon
1	clove garlic, finely minced
¼	cup chopped fresh basil or Italian parsley
½	teaspoon salt
½	cup extra-virgin olive oil
	Freshly ground black pepper

Add rice to boiling stock and turn down to simmer until tender, about 25 minutes. Set aside to cool.

Prepare grill. Wash eggplant and do not peel unless skin is very blemished or seems tough. Slice into ¾-inch-thick rounds. Brush rounds with ¼ cup olive oil until all pieces are well coated. Grill slices until tender. When cool enough to handle, quarter each round into wedges.

Wash and dry radicchio, break into leaves, and brush them with remaining ¼ cup olive oil. Spread on grill and cook quickly, turning once, until radicchio is soft and limp. Slice into strips.

Toss together rice, sliced pepper, and cheese. In a separate bowl, combine lemon, garlic, basil or parsley, salt, and olive oil and mix well. Pour over rice and toss to coat well. Add cooled eggplant and radicchio. Toss gently to avoid mashing eggplant and garnish with plenty of freshly ground black pepper.

Grilled Vegetables with Fried Polenta and Roasted Tomato Dressing

This is a hearty, filling full-meal salad.

Serves 6 to 8

For the Polenta:

3	cups cold water
½	teaspoon salt
½	cup stone-ground cornmeal
½	cup coarse cornmeal or polenta
2	tablespoons grated pecorino romano cheese
1–2	eggs, beaten
1	cup flour
	Olive oil for frying

For the Roasted Tomato Dressing:

7–9	medium-size ripe tomatoes
5	tablespoons olive oil
1	teaspoon minced garlic
½	teaspoon salt
½	teaspoon black pepper
½	teaspoon sugar
2	tablespoons balsamic vinegar

For the grilled vegetables:

2	zucchini
2	yellow squash
1	small eggplant
1	bulb fennel
8	radicchio leaves
	Olive oil
6	ounces low-salt feta cheese, sliced into 8 to 10 pieces
	Fresh basil leaves, optional garnish

Prepare the polenta: Bring 2 cups cold water and the salt to a boil. Combine both cornmeals with 1 cup cold water and stir mixture into boiling water. With a wooden spoon, stir constantly for 10 minutes, or until polenta is thick. Stir in the cheese and mix well. Turn polenta into an oiled 9-inch round cake pan and allow to cool and firm up about 30 minutes (you can chill overnight).

Cut polenta into 8 to 10 pie wedges, coat with egg, then flour, and fry until golden brown on all sides. Drain on paper towel.

Prepare Dressing: Core tomatoes and rub with about 1 tablespoon olive oil. Roast in a high oven until skins brown and burst, about 7-10 minutes.

Heat 2 tablespoons of the olive oil, add garlic and brown. Cook tomatoes until thick, about 20 minutes.

Stir in salt, pepper, sugar, vinegar, and remaining 2 tablespoons olive oil. Set aside.

Grill the vegetables: Prepare grill. Slice the zucchini and squash on the diagonal into wedges. Peel the eggplant, if skin seems tough, and slice into ¹/₂-inch rounds. Cut fennel in half and quarter each half. Rub all the vegetables and radicchio leaves with oil. Cook over grill until slightly tender, but not falling apart. Eggplant will take the longest.

Divide polenta, a scoop of dressing, and grilled vegetables among plates. Top each with a couple of slices of feta cheese and fresh basil leaves, if using.

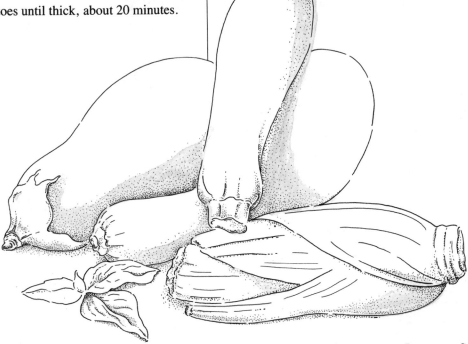

Fresh Corn and Herbed Rice Salad

This salad is "feistier" with the cilantro, but if you can't find any, the parsley works nicely, too. Serve this as a side dish to Mexican tacos, enchiladas, and the like.

Serves 4 to 6

6	**ears cooked corn on the cob**
2	**cups cooked rice**
¼	**cup minced fresh cilantro or Italian parsley**
3	**scallions, thinly sliced**
1	**medium-size tomato, seeded and finely chopped**
	Juice of 2 whole limes
½	**teaspoon salt**
1	**small chili, seeded and minced or ¼ teaspoon crushed red pepper**

Using a sharp knife, slice the kernels of corn from the cob into salad bowl. Combine with all remaining ingredients, toss well, and serve.

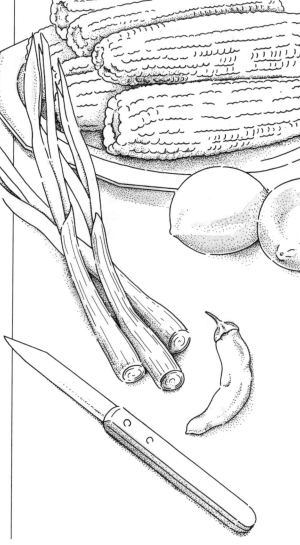

Limas and Turnips with Horseradish Dressing

You can also make this with fresh green peas. It's good picnic or barbecue fare.

Serves 8 to 10

3–4	pounds turnips, peeled and cut into ½-inch dice
½	cup sour cream
½	cup mayonnaise
½	teaspoon salt
2	tablespoons prepared horseradish
2	teaspoons dried dill weed or 1 tablespoon fresh
3	cups cooked lima beans

Drop the turnips in salted boiling water and cook about 5 minutes, until firm-tender. Drain and set aside to cool slightly.

In a large bowl, combine sour cream, mayonnaise, salt, horseradish, and dill, and mix well. Stir in lima beans and cooled turnips and gently mix to coat well. Chill salad for one hour.

Kidney Beans and Escarole

Kidney beans and escarole are both iron-rich foods that go well together.

Serves 4

2	tablespoons fresh lemon juice
2	cloves garlic, minced
½	teaspoon salt
½	teaspoon black pepper
⅓	cup extra-virgin olive oil
2	cups cooked kidney beans
1	small green pepper, chopped
2	medium-size tomatoes, peeled, seeded, and chopped
1	rib celery, finely chopped
6	cups bite-size pieces escarole

In a salad bowl, combine the lemon juice, garlic, salt, black pepper, and oil and mix well. Add the beans, green pepper, tomatoes, celery, and escarole and toss well to coat.

Chick-Pea Medley

Serves 4 to 6

2½   cups cooked chick-peas
1   small fennel bulb, sliced into 2-inch strips
½   pound buffalo-milk or regular mozzarella, cut into ½-inch cubes
½   cup green olives
½   cup black olives
2   tablespoons chopped pimento
1   clove garlic, crushed
1   2-ounce can anchovy fillets, packed in olive oil
⅓   cup white wine vinegar
1   teaspoon dried crumbled oregano
½   teaspoon sugar
½   teaspoon black pepper
⅓   cup olive oil

Combine chick-peas, fennel, mozzarella, olives, and pimento.

In a small bowl, mash together garlic and anchovies with their oil. Stir in remaining ingredients and pour over salad.

Curried Fava and String Bean Salad

Serves 4 to 6

½   cup mayonnaise
¼   cup sour cream
1   tablespoon curry powder
½   teaspoon salt
2   tablespoons chopped fresh cilantro
2   cups cooked fava beans
2   cups cooked string beans, cut diagonally into 2-inch pieces

In a salad bowl, combine the mayonnaise, sour cream, curry powder, salt, and cilantro and mix well. Stir in the fava and string beans and toss to coat.

Tuscan Style Warm Bean Salad (*Fagioli Tuscanelli*)

Serves 6

½	**pound black-eyed peas**
2	**cups dry white wine**
2	**cups water**
4	**tablespoons unsalted butter**
3	**shallots, minced**
2	**cloves garlic, minced**
1	**small sweet red pepper, minced**
4	**tablespoons flour**
1½	**cups reserved cooking liquid**
1	**teaspoon dried crumbled oregano**
¼	**teaspoon crushed red pepper**
1	**teaspoon salt**
2	**tablespoons drained capers**
¼	**cup grated carrot**

Soak peas for 6 hours or overnight. Drain and combine with wine and water. Bring to a boil, then lower heat and simmer for 1 hour, or until tender. Drain, reserving 1½ cups of the cooking liquid.

Heat butter in a saucepan, then add shallots, garlic, and sweet pepper, and cook until soft, about 5 minutes. Stir in flour and form a smooth paste. Then slowly stir in reserved cooking liquid. Add oregano, crushed red pepper, and salt. Cook sauce over low heat until it thickens, about 7 minutes. Stir in capers and carrot, then combine sauce with peas. Allow to cool slightly, but serve warm.

Chapter Four

FRUIT SALADS

Fresh fruit is perfect salad food. Of course, it goes without saying that a good piece of fruit needs no embellishment. But then fruit, with its color, texture, and overall visual appeal lends itself to fanciful presentation from simple and elegant to the elaborately flamboyant. In some cases, rinds, shells, and outer coverings can be hollowed and carved into pretty bowls and containers for cut-up fruit and its dressing. Fruits can be sculpted by a deft and patient hand into all manner of artistry.

Use only the best fruit at peak ripeness. Overly ripe fruit may taste great, but it will lose its form and "muddy up" a good salad. An exception to this rule is for persimmons, which are almost never good to eat until very soft-ripe. (There is an exception to this exception—the fuyu persimmon grown in California; it is eaten at a crisp stage of ripeness.) For this reason, don't add fruit such as very ripe persimmons, bananas, or pears to a mixed fruit salad. Rather, decorate a big platter with slices, wedges, or rounds of the fruit, enhanced with a few drops of lemon or lime juice, some crème fraiche, sour cream, or yogurt, or just a light sprinkling of nutmeg or cinnamon. Fresh persimmon slices (or fresh peaches, nectarines, or apples) and a scoop of cottage cheese are a wonderful updated variation on an old stodgy theme.

Some fruits discolor quickly and should be eaten soon after being cut. A squeeze of lemon or lime juice will keep most cut fruit from browning too quickly. Most fruit salads taste best when served well chilled, not at room temperature, as I have recommended for other types of salads.

Dressings for fruit salads should take into account the fruit's own juice or degree of sweetness, which becomes an integral part of the dressing. Do you want to play up or play down the fruit's tart or sweet attributes? Sugar, honey, some fruit juices (such as grape and apple) can blunt the edge of tartness. An acid—lemon or lime juice, or various vinegars—will foil the fruit's natural sweetness and make for a better savory salad, rather than dessert dish.

Fruit has long been considered one of nature's best digestive aids. So a fruit salad can be a savory composition that prepares the palate for a bigger, richer meal to come. Or it can be the centerpiece, thus the more filling component of a breakfast, brunch, or lunch menu. It can sometimes be a dessert salad that simply cleanses and tops off a good meal.

Fruit mingled with meat, fish, and fowl has long been favored in many parts of the world and is now more revered in American cooking. The sweetness, tanginess, and texture of many fruits is a good complement for most meat and fish.

FRUIT SALAD TIPS

• When combining fruits, consider a balance of tartness and sweetness, of sharp and bland. Strawberries and citrus fruit, for example, are sharp and tart. So, mix such fruits with fruits such as bananas, pears, or papayas, which are sweet, mellow, and bland.

• Consider texture, too. Try to mix fruits that complement each other with a variety of soft and crunchy, delicate and crisp.

• Be careful when mixing fruits with vegetables. Consider tart, sour, mild, bland aspects to keep a pleasant balance.

• Tart, sharp fruits and dark, leafy greens mix well together. Just be sure the dressing is not too sharp or acidic.

• Creamy dressings based on sour cream, crème fraiche, and heavy cream are often good dressings for fruit salads. Yogurt is good, too, though it may require some sweetening with sugar or fruit juice to lessen its sourness.

• Vinaigrettes spiked and sweetened with a fruit juice are good dressing for fruit and vegetable salads.

• Although it is ideal to rely on a fruit's natural sweetness, sometimes the addition of a little sugar can stave off too much sourness. Use extra-fine sugar for fruit salads, because it dissolves faster.

Note that fruit is excellent set into jelled salads. Such preparations are discussed in the next section on molded salads, pages 100 to 105.

CUTTING FRUIT

Here are some guidelines for cutting some fruits used in salads:

Apples. Core apples before peeling them. To core: insert the tip of the corer into the stem end of the apple first, pushing the corer about halfway through the apple. Twist to loosen the core. Repeat from the bottom end, twisting and pushing until the core can be pushed out the opposite end.

Mangoes. Mangoes have a large, flat-ridged tenacious stone at the center of their flesh. To get the most flesh for your effort you can attack mangoes in either of two ways—with or without its peel. If the mango is particularly ripe and soft, do not peel first. With a sharp knife, make a vertical slash from stem to bottom, down to the stone. About an inch from the first gash, slice another parallel gash diagonally toward the stone to free up a slice of mango. Then, if not peeled, slice the flesh from the peel. You can repeat this procedure until you have freed up most of the flesh. If firm, you can peel the mango first, then proceed to free up the flesh in the same manner.

Papaya. Unless the papaya is very ripe and soft, peel it first either with a vegetable parer or sharp paring knife. Then slice the papaya in half, cutting through the middle of the womblike hollow, which is packed with pearly gray seeds. The seeds, which have a peppery flavor, may be crushed and used to spice up vinaigrette dressings, or simply added whole to sliced crescents of papaya. After halving the papaya, slice and cut to desired size.

Mangoes

Papaya

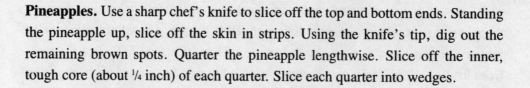

Pineapples. Use a sharp chef's knife to slice off the top and bottom ends. Standing the pineapple up, slice off the skin in strips. Using the knife's tip, dig out the remaining brown spots. Quarter the pineapple lengthwise. Slice off the inner, tough core (about ¼ inch) of each quarter. Slice each quarter into wedges.

Oranges, Grapefruits. Citrus to be used in fruit salads are usually peeled with a sharp paring knife, so that you can remove most of the pith as well as skin. Sometimes you may want to remove the membrane also. In this case cut even more deeply into the fruit. Then free the sections from the core with the knife by cutting down on both sides of each section. Work over a bowl to catch the juice.

Greens, Pears, and Gorgonzola with Champagne-Hazelnut Dressing

Serves 4 to 6

2	ripe Anjou pears
1/3	cup champagne vinegar
1/4	teaspoon Dijon mustard
1/2	teaspoon salt
1/2	teaspoon freshly ground black pepper
1/4	cup mild-flavored oil (a light olive, corn, or safflower oil)
2	tablespoons hazelnut oil
6	cups mixed bite-size pieces strong and mild greens, such as arugula, red- and greenleaf, butter, radicchio, and limestone lettuces
4	ounces imported gorgonzola cheese Freshly ground black pepper

Peel, halve, and core pears. Slice each half into thin slices. Combine vinegar, mustard, salt, pepper, and oils in a salad bowl. Toss in greens and coat well with dressing. Divide greens among 4 to 6 salad plates and top each one with pear slices. Overlap the pear slices in the shape of a fan. Crumble some cheese over each serving. Garnish with few grinds black pepper.

Waldorf Slaw with Fresh Mandarins

This is a variation on the classic celery, walnut, and mayonnaise salad, which was invented some years ago by a chef at the Waldorf Astoria Hotel. This recipe makes about 1 quart, enough for a picnic crowd or 8 to 10 as a side dish.

1   medium-size head green cabbage, shredded
3   stalks celery, with some leaves, sliced (about 2 cups)
1½   cups walnut halves
1   cup currants
2   egg yolks
⅓   cup olive oil
2   tablespoons fresh lemon juice
4   tablespoons orange juice
⅓   cup vegetable oil
2   tablespoons walnut oil
2   teaspoons ground coriander
1   teaspoon salt
3   fresh mandarins, peeled and sectioned

Combine cabbage, celery, walnuts, and currants in a large salad bowl.

With a wire whisk, beat egg yolks in a medium-size bowl until lemon yellow. Very slowly beat in the olive oil. The sauce will become very thick as it emulsifies. Slowly beat in alternately the lemon and orange juices and remaining oils, being careful not to curdle sauce. If dressing is becoming too thin, do not add remaining orange juice.

Stir coriander and salt into sauce and toss with cabbage mixture. You can add mandarin sections as decoration on top of salad or as garnish on individual servings.

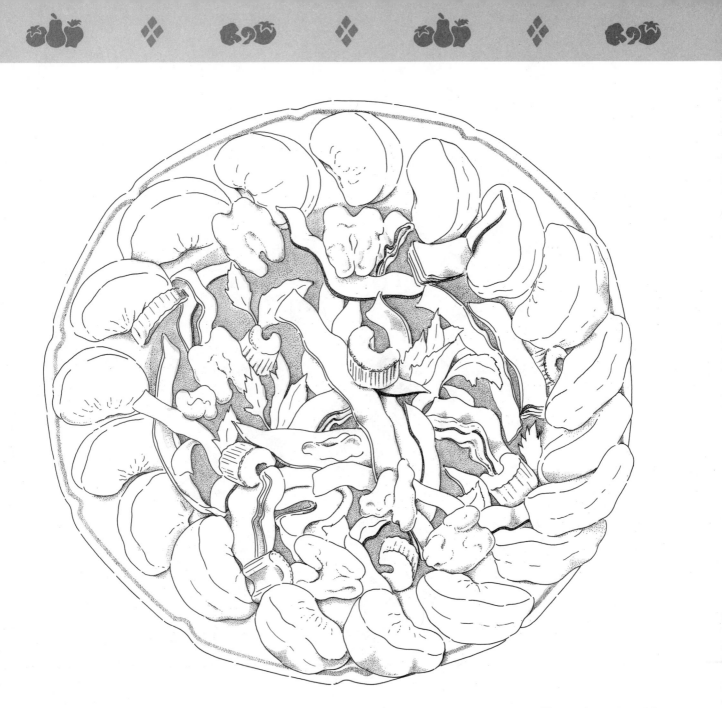

Green Mango Salad with Sprouts

This is a delicious and easy salad to make, especially refreshing in summer as an appetizer or side dish to any meat or fowl entrée. Don't worry if your mangoes are slightly ripened and not very green—just so long as they are fairly firm.

Serves 4 to 6

2   medium-size green or barely ripe mangoes, pitted, skinned, and diced
1   cup fresh mung bean sprouts
     Juice of 2 whole limes
¼   cup Thai fish sauce*
1   tablespoon hot chili oil* or ½ teaspoon crushed red pepper
     Whole lettuce leaves (loose-leaf, butter, or romaine)
4   tablespoons chopped cilantro
3   cloves garlic, chopped and sautéed until crispy brown

Combine mangoes, sprouts, lime juice, fish sauce, and chili oil (or red pepper) and toss. Place salad on a bed of lettuce leaves and garnish with cilantro and garlic.

*Available at Asian food markets.

Curried Papaya and Chicken

Serves 6

1   large firm, ripe papaya
1½   pounds boneless, skinned chicken breast, cooked and cut into bite-size pieces
½   cup chopped celery
2   tablespoons minced onion
½   cup Orange Curry Mayonnaise, page 120
6   large firm lettuce leaves
2   tablespoons chopped fresh cilantro

Peel the papaya and cut it in half. Remove and discard the seeds. Slice the papaya into ½-inch-by-1½-inch strips.

Toss the chicken, celery, and onion with the mayonnaise. Add the papaya strips and toss gently. Pile each serving on a lettuce leaf, then garnish with some cilantro.

Spicy Pork and Apple Salad

Serves 4 as an appetizer

For the pork:

2	tablespoons minced garlic
2	tablespoons minced fresh ginger
3	tablespoons soy sauce
1	tablespoon lime juice
½	cup canned coconut milk
1	tablespoon brown sugar
⅛	teaspoon cayenne pepper
½	pound lean boneless pork, cut into thin strips
3	tablespoons peanut oil
1	tart green apple, cored and chopped
2	cups shredded napa cabbage

Dressing:

3	tablespoons soy sauce
2	tablespoons lemon juice
1	teaspoon grated ginger
½	teaspoon minced garlic
1	teaspoon sugar
2	tablespoons chopped fresh cilantro

Prepare the pork: Combine garlic, ginger, soy sauce, lime juice, coconut milk, sugar, and pepper and mix well. Stir in pork strips and marinate at least 1 hour.

Heat oil in a skillet or wok. Add pork with a couple tablespoons of marinade and cook until lightly browned. With a slotted spoon transfer pork to a salad bowl and add apple and cabbage.

Mix dressing ingredients and toss with salad.

Pepino and Prosciutto Appetizer

The pepino, a sort of melon, made its appearance in our produce markets—from New Zealand—almost ten years ago and is more and more available. It is delicate and delicious when properly ripe. If you can't find pepinos, use any kind of melon or Anjou pears instead.

Serves 4

4 thin slices prosciutto
2 medium-size pepinos, cut into thin slices
1 roasted sweet red pepper, cut into thin strips
1/2 pound fresh mozzarella, sliced
1/2 cup oil-cured black olives
2 tablespoons extra-virgin olive oil
 Freshly ground black pepper

Roll the prosciutto slices into small cylinders and arrange with pepino slices, roasted pepper, cheese, and olives on a platter in pinwheel fashion. Sprinkle the olive oil and black pepper over all contents of platter.

Mango and Avocado with Hearts of Escarole

You can also use chicory or romaine lettuce.

Serves 4

3–4 hearts (light green and yellow inner portion) of escarole, cut into bite-size pieces
1 firm, ripe avocado, peeled and sliced
1 firm, ripe mango, peeled and sliced
1/2 cup toasted nut halves (walnuts, pecans, or hazelnuts)
2 tablespoons orange juice
2 tablespoons lime juice
1 tablespoon white wine vinegar
1/3 cup olive oil
1/2 teaspoon salt
1/4 teaspoon ground ginger
1/4 teaspoon ground coriander

Combine the hearts of escarole, avocado, mango, and nuts in a salad bowl and toss gently to mix. Place the remaining ingredients in a blender and process until smoothly mixed. Pour over the salad and toss again gently to coat ingredients.

Pears, Nuts, and Romaine with Raspberry Vinaigrette

Serves 4 to 6

2	firm, ripe Anjou or bosc pears
1	head romaine lettuce, washed and torn into bite-size pieces
½	cup coarsely chopped, toasted walnuts
¼	cup dried currants
¼	cup raspberry vinegar
⅓	cup olive oil
2	tablespoons walnut oil
½	teaspoon sugar
½	teaspoon salt
½	teaspoon black pepper

Peel, halve, and core the pears. Slice the halves thinly and then cut the slices in half lengthwise. Toss the pears with the lettuce, nuts, and currants.

Combine the remaining dressing ingredients and mix well. Pour over salad and toss to coat well.

Italian-Style Oranges and Redleaf Lettuce

This works best with a thick, fruity, green olive oil and juicy seedless oranges that are slightly tart.

Serves 4

2	medium-size tart-sweet oranges
1	head redleaf lettuce, cleaned and kept in large pieces
4	tablespoons extra-virgin olive oil
½	teaspoon salt
	Freshly ground black pepper

With a sharp paring knife, slice off the top and bottom ends of the oranges, then slice the remaining peel, removing as much of the pith as possible. Cut the oranges into ¼-inch-thick rounds. Toss the oranges and lettuce together. Sprinkle the olive oil, salt, and a copious amount of fresh black pepper over the salad and toss with your hands.

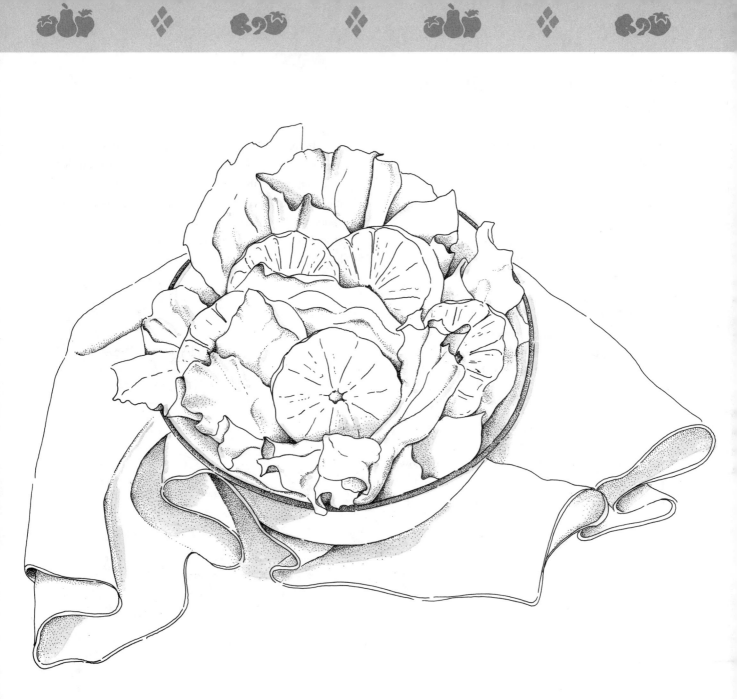

Mixed Summer Fruit with Yogurt Cheese

Note that you need two days to prepare the yogurt cheese.

Serves 4 to 6

1   **2-pound container of plain yogurt**
2   **pints fresh strawberries, washed and stemmed**
¼   **cup extra fine sugar**
1   **tablespoon lemon juice**
2   **firm-ripe bananas, peeled and sliced**
3   **ripe peaches, peeled and sliced**
1   **cup fresh blueberries, washed**
     Fresh mint leaves

Line a colander with paper coffee filters (split open and overlapped) or strong paper toweling. Place the yogurt in the colander and position over a bowl or pot to catch the dripping whey. Allow to drain for two days in the refrigerator. Discard whey when done.

Puree 1 pint of the strawberries with the sugar and lemon juice. Slice the other pint of strawberries in half and combine with the bananas, peaches, and blueberries. To serve: Place fruit salad in bowls, and spoon some yogurt cheese on top of each serving. Pour strawberry sauce on top. Garnish with fresh mint leaves.

Nectarines with Creamy Papaya Dressing

This is refreshing as a breakfast salad in summertime or as part of a light lunch.

Serves 4

½   cup sour cream (or ¼ cup sour cream and ¼ cup plain yogurt)
½   cup papaya nectar*
3   medium to large ripe nectarines, sliced
       Cinnamon and nutmeg
       Sprigs of watercress or fresh mint

Blend the sour cream and papaya nectar and toss with the nectarine slices. Sprinkle a little cinnamon and nutmeg on each serving and garnish with a sprig of watercress or mint.
*Available at natural food or health food stores.

DESSERT FRUIT SALADS

The following fruit salads are sweet enough to serve as dessert salads, yet they are still lighter than most desserts. Serve them at the end of a rich meal or include them in a brunch or lunch menu.

Peaches and Strawberries with Almond Dressing

If fruit is particularly tart, add a little more sugar to dressing.

Serves 4 to 6

½   cup almond butter*
2   tablespoons brandy
½   cup heavy cream
2   tablespoons sugar
4   large ripe peaches, peeled and sliced
2   cups fresh strawberries, washed, de-stemmed, and sliced

Combine almond butter, brandy, cream, and sugar in a blender and process until smooth.
Arrange peaches and strawberries on a platter and pour dressing over them.
*Available in health food stores.

Arugula and Blood Oranges with Triple Sec

At one time you had to travel to a Mediterranean country to find these beautiful ruby- and gold-fleshed fruits. Now most markets carry them in season—spring.

Serves 4

5–6   medium-size blood oranges
1   head of arugula
⅓   cup Triple Sec
2   teaspoons extra-fine sugar
2   tablespoons hazelnut or walnut oil

With a small sharp knife, pare the oranges, removing all pith. Slice them thinly in rounds.

Clean and dry the arugula and keep the leaves whole. Remove any tough stems. Toss with the oranges.

Combine the Triple Sec and sugar and stir. Add the oil and stir again. Sprinkle over salad and toss to coat.

Persimmons with Sake

Persimmons are at their peak in the fall. They will ripen to pudding-sweet texture. Storing them in a brown bag at room temperature hastens their ripening.

Serves 4

3–4   ripe persimmons
2   teaspoons extra-fine sugar
½   cup sake
1   tablespoon chopped candied ginger
      Fresh mint leaves

With a very sharp knife, slice persimmons into rounds and arrange, overlapping on a platter. Sprinkle evenly with sugar, then with sake. Garnish with ginger and mint.

Fresh Figs with Raspberries and Amaretto

Serves 4

10   fresh green and/or purple figs
2   cups fresh raspberries
½   cup amaretto
2   teaspoons sugar

Wash, stem, and quarter figs lengthwise. Gently rinse raspberries and spread on paper towel to absorb all moisture. Combine with figs in a bowl.

Heat amaretto with sugar in small saucepan, just until sugar is dissolved, about 5 minutes. Cool slightly and sprinkle over fruit. Toss and serve.

Chapter Five

MOLDED SALADS

Molded salad almost sounds like an oxymoron. There is something so random, loose, and free-form sounding to the word *salad* and something structured, definitive, and rigid to the idea of mold. Yet it works: A salad suspended diaphanously in a glistening, translucent jelly or aspic makes for a bit of drama in presentation.

Meats, fish, fowl, vegetables, fruits, nuts, fresh herbs—just about anything can be shaped into a mold. They make fine centerpieces for luncheon menus or for hot and cold buffets. Use your imagination in garnishing and serving the mold. Place it on a bed of crisp greens strewn with some edible flowers or colorful fruit.

An aspic is a jelly made from reduced chicken or veal stock. Fish and meat stock can be used, too. If using canned stock (which is perfectly fine), choose the more lightly salted brands, so that you can salt to taste.

Usually by molded salads we mean one formed from gelatin. But I include one here that is a rice mold made without gelatin. You can find pretty decorative molds that fit the theme of the food or meal—a fish mold for fish aspic, a cornucopia for a fruit mold, for example. If the mold is not a clear one, you can lightly oil the mold to help remove it when firm. (The oil drops may hinder the appearance of a clear mold.)

MOLDED SALAD TIPS

• Serve gelatin molds well chilled.

• Never freeze molded salads.

• Do not oversalt molds, as the salt can break down the gelatin's staying power.

• In general, use about 1 tablespoon of gelatin per 2 to 3 cups of liquid, depending on the juiciness or water content of ingredients to go into the mold. One package of gelatin equals 1 tablespoon.

• Never add fresh pineapple, figs, kiwi, or papaya to gelatins. They have enzymes that inhibit the jelling action.

• To unmold firm gelatins, turn the mold onto a plate, then place a towel soaked in hot water over the mold, until the gelatin drops onto the plate.

• For a buffet presentation, serve gelatin molds on a chilled platter set over ice.

Lobster Crab Mousse

Use a nice decorative fish mold for this lovely centerpiece.

Serves 6

2	tablespoons gelatin
1	cup fish stock
½	cup clam juice
8	ounces cooked crab meat
6	ounces cooked lobster meat
1	cup heavy cream
1	4-ounce package cream cheese
1	teaspoon salt
2	tablespoons tarragon vinegar
¼	cup finely chopped scallions
2	tablespoons chopped fresh chives
2	tablespoons chopped fresh parsley
½	teaspoon crushed red pepper flakes

Soften gelatin in ½ cup stock. Heat remaining stock and clam juice over low heat and stir in softened gelatin until dissolved, about 5 minutes. Chill mixture until slightly thickened, about 45 minutes.

Meanwhile, blend crab, lobster, cream, cream cheese, and salt together in a food processor, fitted with the metal blade (mixture may be too chunky to blend well in a blender). Add thickened gelatin, vinegar, scallions, chives, parsley, and pepper and process just until blended evenly.

Pour mixture into a 1-quart oiled mold and chill at least 6 hours. Turn out onto a serving platter.

Mexican Confetti Rice Mold with Spicy Mexican Dressing

Serves 4 to 6 as main dish

4	cups vegetable or meat stock
2	cups long-grain brown rice
½	teaspoon turmeric
3	tablespoons vegetable oil
1	sweet red pepper, chopped
½	teaspoon ground cumin
4	scallions, thinly sliced
10	button mushrooms, sliced
1	cup frozen corn
1	cup shredded purple cabbage
⅔	cup sliced black olives
3	tablespoons chopped fresh cilantro
2	medium-size tomatoes, seeded and diced
	Salt and pepper
	Spicy Mexican Dressing, page 113
½	cup sour cream

Bring stock to a boil. Add rice and turmeric, lower heat, cover and simmer until rice is cooked, about 25 minutes.

Meanwhile, heat oil and add red pepper and cumin. Sauté 3 minutes over moderate heat. Add scallions, mushrooms, and corn. Stir and cook 5 minutes. Stir in cabbage and remove from heat.

When cooked rice has cooled slightly, stir in vegetable mixture, olives, cilantro, and tomatoes. Taste and correct seasoning. Press into a 5- to 7-cup mold and chill for 1 hour or longer.

Combine Spicy Mexican Dressing with sour cream. Unmold salad and pour dressing over individual servings.

Cranberry, Orange, and Nut Mold

Serves 4 to 6

1	tablespoon gelatin
¼	cup water
3	cups fresh cranberries
1¼	cups orange juice
½	cup sugar
½	cup chopped celery or chopped fresh fennel
½	cup grated unsweetened coconut
1	orange, peeled and chopped
⅓	cup coarsely chopped walnuts
¼	cup Grand Marnier
½	pint cream, whipped

Dissolve gelatin in water.

Simmer the cranberries in the orange juice until their skins burst, about 3 minutes. Add the sugar and softened gelatin and cook 3 minutes longer over low heat to dissolve. Stir in celery or fennel, coconut, orange, and walnuts. Pour into a 1½- to 2-quart mold and chill until firm.

Unmold salad onto platter. Combine Grand Marnier with whipped cream and serve on top of mold.

Cream of Gazpacho Mold

Serves 6 to 8

3	cups very ripe tomatoes, finely chopped (or 3 cups canned tomatoes with juice)
¼	cup minced onion
2	cloves garlic, minced
1	rib celery with leaves, finely chopped
1	small green pepper, chopped
1	teaspoon salt
1	teaspoon sugar
½	teaspoon black pepper
2	tablespoons fresh lemon juice
¼	cup chopped parsley
½	cucumber, peeled and finely chopped
2	tablespoons gelatin
¼	cup tomato juice or water
½	cup heavy cream
	Leaves of watercress

Simmer tomatoes, onions, garlic, celery, green pepper, salt, sugar, and black pepper for 25 minutes. Remove from heat, add lemon juice, parsley, and cucumber, and set aside.

In a small saucepan, combine gelatin and tomato juice or water and allow to soften for 3 minutes, then heat until gelatin is dissolved. Pour the gelatin into the vegetable mixture along with cream and mix well. Pour into an oiled 1-quart ring mold and chill until firm. Unmold onto a plate and fill the center with watercress leaves.

Salmon, Shrimp, and Dill Aspic

Serves 4 to 6

2	tablespoons gelatin
2	cups rich stock
¹/₂	pound salmon
2	cups clam juice
	Juice of 1 whole lemon
¹/₄	pound cooked baby shrimp
	Fresh dill sprigs
	Mixed greens

Soften gelatin in ¹/₂ cup of the stock. Bring remaining stock to a boil and add salmon. Remove from heat, cover, and let sit for 10 to 15 minutes, just until salmon is cooked through. Remove salmon with a slotted spoon and cut into 1-inch pieces. Cover and refrigerate.

Strain stock. Return to heat. Stir in softened gelatin, clam juice, and lemon juice, and reheat to dissolve gelatin. Chill gelatin until it is just about to set, about 1 to 1¹/₂ hours. Combine it with salmon, shrimp, and dill sprigs and pour into a 1-quart mold. Chill until firm. Unmold and serve on a bed of greens.

White Wine Jelly and Fruit

Serves 6 to 8

2	tablespoons gelatin
¹/₂	cup water
3	cups chardonnay or other dry white wine
	Juice of 2 whole limes
²/₃	cup sugar
2	pints fresh strawberries, stemmed and sliced
2	bananas, sliced

Soften the gelatin in the water. Heat the wine, lime juice, and sugar and simmer for about 5 minutes until sugar is dissolved. Add gelatin and simmer another 5 minutes. Pour into a 1- to 1¹/₂-quart mold and chill until syrupy, about 1¹/₂ to 2 hours. Add sliced fruit and chill thoroughly. Unmold and serve with plain yogurt or sour cream.

Variation: Use 3 cups of sliced peaches in place of the strawberries and bananas.

Chapter Six

SALAD DRESSINGS

Although all the ingredients must cooperate equally, for many salads it is the dressing that defines the prominent flavoring and adds the dominant character. The dressing—more so than any other ingredient—can make or break a salad.

Keep in mind that a dressing can be as basic as a squirt of lemon or lime juice, a few drops of vinegar, or a splash of an aromatic or seasoned oil.

Most salad dressings are either vinaigrettes (vinegar and oil), mayonnaise-based, or creamy (based on yogurt, sour cream, crème fraiche, buttermilk, or cream). But there is a whole spectrum of variations between each type. And, as I have already said, we have gotten quite free with our interpretation of salad dressing; You will find here some new types such as Tapenade Dressing, Tomato-Tamari Dressing, and Spicy Indonesian Dressing.

A fresh green salad should never swim in its dressing. The greens should just be coated so they glisten, thus not upstaging their flavor.

In some cases you may find it easier to mix the dressing in the bottom of the salad bowl before adding and tossing the salad. At other times, you may want to keep both the dressing and salad pre-mixed but separate until serving time. In this case you may mix the dressing in a small bowl or a jar.

Most dressings are best when made fresh. This is especially true for the vinaigrette dressings made with oils and vinegars that owe their character and charm to volatile, easily diminished elements. But some dressings do keep well for a short time. Mayonnaise and creamy dressings, of course, should always be refrigerated. If you do have a leftover vinaigrette, it may be refrigerated, too, or kept at room temperature for a few days.

SALAD OILS

We have certainly come a long way since the days when oil was a pale, bland liquid, adding little more than lubrication and calories to our food. Now, we find oils that offer taste, tint, and bouquet with the same nuances of fine wines.

The overwhelming oil of choice for many of today's salad chefs is a good olive oil. Extra-virgin is the best quality olive oil, virgin is next in line, and pure olive oil is the most refined, the cheapest, and imparts the least olive flavor. The degree of fruitiness can vary greatly and is a matter of personal preference. A "flexible" rule of thumb is that the dark green olive oils are sharper and stronger, while the lighter and golden olive oils are rounder and more mellow. The best advice on olive oil is to shop around until you find one that suits your taste.

Note that many recipes in this book call for extra-virgin or just olive oil. The latter is specified when the quality is not so important—extra-virgin is the most costly—and when a less pronounced olive flavor is desirable. It is rare to find virgin olive oil in this country, so I have not specified its use in any recipes, but it is perfectly fine to use if you find some you like.

You can also mix different-strength olive oils or olive oil and a mild vegetable-flavored oil, such as peanut to achieve a desired taste.

Most good oils such as robust hazelnut or buttery walnut have undergone minimal processing and refinement, which preserves the native flavor, aroma, and color of the original nut, seed, or fruit source. Nowhere in this book will you find the tasteless supermarket product that has been treated to high-heat pressing, chemical solvents, alkali solutions, bleaching agents, and deodorizing that neutralizes away all character. You can use such oil, but it won't add much of anything memorable to your salad.

Here are some guidelines for using the highly flavored oils (many of which can now be found even in the large supermarkets—sometimes in the specialty foods section):

• Buy specialty oils in small amounts, since they are more prone to rancidity than highly refined oils. That is, from the moment the oil's seal is broken and oxygen is introduced, decomposition of the oil's volatile elements, which form their unique flavors, begins.

• You can store good oils at room temperature if you intend to use them within about six months. For longer storage you can refrigerate oils to slow down deterioration, especially if the container is opened. Some clouding in cold storage is natural and will dissipate at room temperature.

• It's a good idea to test the strength of an oil that is new to your palate. Test it with a few greens to see if you want to cut it with a milder oil. Almond, hazelnut, and walnut oils can be robust and are good on arugula, watercress, radicchio, and the chicories. If you find these oils too strong, cut them with a little avocado oil, which is nutty also, but much milder.

OIL GLOSSARY

Almond. Mildly sweet and nutty; very light if refined. It is good for strong-flavored greens.

Avocado. Has a sweet walnutlike flavor. It is a good vinaigrette dressing for most greens. Mixed with a few drops of fresh lemon or lime juice, it is nice on bitter greens, such as arugula, chicory, and watercress.

Corn. Light and bland, with hints of corn flavor. It may be used where a vegetable oil is called for or for cutting the more pungent and strongly flavored oils, such as olive and hazelnut.

Hazelnut. Rich and robust, very strong flavored. It is often cut somewhat with a mild olive oil. It is great on sharply flavored greens.

Olive. Can be light to very fruity and peppery. It is great on strong-flavored greens, pasta salads, and meat, fowl, or fish salads. (Please see above for more discussion on olive oil.)

Peanut. Distinctly peanutty, it is good alone or mixed with other oils.

Safflower. Bland and light, but can be used to cut strong-flavored oils for dressings. It is considered an especially healthy oil because of its linoleic acid (a polyunsaturated fat) richness.

Sunflower. A mild hint of raw sunflower seeds. May be used when a mild vegetable oil is called for.

Walnut. A rich butternut flavor good in dressings with fruit-flavored vinegars for sharp or sweet greens.

VINEGARS

Adding vinegar is one of the oldest ways to season foods. Vinegar has long been a crucial adding element in marinades, pickles, relishes, and many saladlike condiments. All vinegars, which are actually intentionally soured wines, have a preservative quality because of their 4 to 7 percent acidity. Like wines, vinegar too can be mellow, sharp, sour, or sweet. Vinegars owe their traits largely to their source and to fermentation techniques. Some are so fine that they can be used alone as the sole seasoning on a fresh salad. Just go slowly, as it's easy to overdo with vinegar. Make sure the vinegar amplifies, rather than overpowers, the salad you are dressing.

VINEGAR GLOSSARY

Balsamic vinegar. Produced in Modena, Italy, balsamic vinegar has 6 percent acidity. It is dark and flavorful—sweet and woodsy—thanks to its long aging period. It is great on pungent greens, roasted meat, or cooked fish salads. It works great as a sole seasoning or with olive or nut oils.

Champagne wine vinegar. Six to seven percent acidity. Champagne wine vinegar may be distilled in France from champagne or chardonnay wine. It is slightly fruitier than white wine vinegar and can be used in the same way.

Cider vinegar. Fermented from apple juice, cider vinegar is about five to six percent acid and has a pronounced apple-acid flavor. It is good in marinades for vegetables and also in salad dressings and condiments, especially those with strong or aromatic ingredients, such as soy sauce, dill, or tomatoes. It goes well with peanut or sesame oils.

Rice vinegar. Distilled from rice, rice vinegar has less sharpness than cider vinegar and a hint of sweetness. The Japanese use rice vinegar to make sushi, dipping sauces, and many pickled dishes. It is good in Oriental salads with tofu and also in grain and bean salads.

Sherry wine vinegar. Distilled from sherry, the best coming from Spain, where this spirit originates. Sherry wine vinegar is aged in oak casks. It has about six percent acidity, is robust and malty and very expensive. Its caramel richness should be used with restraint, in much the same way as balsamic vinegar.

Wine vinegars. With about five percent acetic acid content, wine vinegars may be derived from red, white, or rosé wines. They are robust and perceptibly fruity and go well with green salads. Red wine vinegar is the traditional choice for Italian dressings. White wine vinegar is slightly more delicate and is often infused with an herb or spice, or used as the basis for fruit vinegars.

FLAVORING YOUR OWN VINEGARS AND OILS

You can easily steep herbs and spices in vinegars and oils, suspending their essence for use in marinades and salad dressings. Make your own aromatic infusion by choosing a single herb—basil, tarragon, rosemary, for example—or a mixed bouquet, adding garlic, peppercorns, cinnamon sticks, ginger, coriander seeds, or any spice blend. Place the vinegar or oil (olive oil is a good choice) and fresh herbs and spices in bottles with clamp-type caps or tightfitting corks.

Raspberry Vinegar

Berry and fruit vinegars add a pleasant tart sweetness to fruit, vegetable, poultry, or fish salads. You can easily make your own.

2   cups white wine vinegar
2   tablespoons sugar
1   cup fresh raspberries (you may substitute any other berries)

Combine vinegar and sugar and heat almost to boiling, just until sugar is dissolved.

Place berries and vinegar in a jar with a tight-fitting non-corrosive lid. Cool before sealing tightly. Allow to steep several days before using.

Red Wine Vinaigrette

This is a great all-time standard for many green salads.

Makes ³/₄ cup

¹/₄   cup red wine vinegar
¹/₂   teaspoon salt
¹/₂   teaspoon black pepper

1   small clove garlic, very finely minced
¹/₄   cup extra-virgin olive oil
¹/₄   cup peanut oil

Mix vinegar, salt, pepper, and garlic and stir gently. Stir in oils, but do not agitate or overmix.

Sweet Balsamic Vinaigrette

Makes about ³/₄ cup

¹/₄   cup balsamic vinegar
1   teaspoon sugar
¹/₂   teaspoon salt
¹/₂   teaspoon black pepper
¹/₂   cup extra-virgin olive oil

Combine vinegar, sugar, salt, and pepper in a jar and shake well. Add olive oil and shake well again.

Variations: Add 2 tablespoons chopped sun-dried tomatoes—they add more sweetness. Or, add several drops hot pepper oil for a nice piquancy.

Spicy Mexican Dressing

Makes about ¾ cup

2	tablespoons red wine vinegar
1	teaspoon fresh lemon juice
1	tablespoon minced red onion
1	tablespoon chipotle paste (see below)
¼	cup chopped fresh or canned tomatoes
½	teaspoon salt
1	teaspoon sugar
½	cup olive oil

Place all ingredients in a jar and shake well.

Chipotle Paste

You can refrigerate this paste for several months or freeze for longer. Use gloves when handling these hot peppers, as they can irritate skin and eyes.

Makes about ½ cup

16	medium-size dried chipotles

Soak the chipotles overnight in enough water to cover. Drain and reserve about ½ cup liquid. Remove stems and puree with reserved liquid or ½ cup tomato juice (for a bit milder taste).

Herbed French Dressing

Makes ³/₄ cup

¹/₄	cup white wine vinegar
1	teaspoon Dijon mustard
¹/₂	teaspoon salt
¹/₄	teaspoon white pepper
1	teaspoon each of any 3 of the following fresh herbs: thyme, Italian parsley, tarragon, basil, or chervil
¹/₂	cup olive or walnut oil

Combine vinegar, mustard, salt, pepper, and herbs in a jar and shake well. Stir in oil and mix well again.

Toasted Pine Nut Basil Dressing

Makes about ³/₄ cup

2	tablespoons toasted pine nuts
¹/₄	cup white wine vinegar
¹/₂	cup olive oil
¹/₂	teaspoon sugar
¹/₄	teaspoon salt
¹/₄	teaspoon black pepper
1	tablespoon minced fresh basil

Gently crush 1 tablespoon pine nuts, just to break nuts. Do not pound to a meal. Combine all remaining ingredients and mix well.

Tapenade Dressing

This dark, rich dressing is great on any green, tossed with some tomatoes and cucumbers. It's also an excellent dressing for a pasta salad—try orzo or penne.

Makes about ³/₄ cup

¼   cup dry-cured, pitted olives (about 18 small olives)
2   tablespoons balsamic vinegar
2   tablespoons red wine vinegar
½   teaspoon sugar
2   teaspoons drained capers
1   clove garlic
½   cup olive oil
    Black pepper, to taste

Puree all ingredients in a blender.

Toasted Sesame Dressing

Makes 1¹/₂ cups

2   tablespoons toasted sesame seeds
½   teaspoon salt
½   cup rice or cider vinegar
2   tablespoons soy sauce
2   tablespoons sherry
²/₃ cup peanut oil

Crush or pound sesame seeds slightly with salt. Combine with vinegar, soy sauce, and sherry and mix well. Add oil and mix well.

Serving suggestions: Use this dressing on 3 to 4 cups of chilled steamed vegetables, such as broccoli, cauliflower, yellow squash, zucchini, and snow peas.

Tomato-Tamari Dressing

Tamari is a type of naturally fermented soy sauce found in any health food store. You can use any type of soy sauce for this recipe, but tamari, with its deeper, richer, more pungent flavor is the soy of choice. This is especially nice with cubes of fresh tofu and firm dark greens.

Makes 1¼ cups

½   cup crushed fresh or canned tomatoes
¼   cup tamari soy sauce
2   tablespoons red wine vinegar
¾   cup peanut or safflower oil

Combine tomatoes, tamari, and vinegar. Strain mixture through a metal strainer to remove pulp and seeds. Combine tamari mixture with oil and mix well.

Mild Salsa Dressing

This dressing tastes best at room temperature, not chilled.

Makes 1¾ cups

4   plump ripe tomatoes
1   Anaheim (or other mild) chili, roasted, peeled, seeded, and finely chopped

2   tablespoons minced green onions
2   tablespoons olive oil
½   teaspoon minced garlic
     Juice of 1 whole lime
2   tablespoons chopped fresh cilantro
½   teaspoon black pepper
½   teaspoon salt

Drop tomatoes carefully into boiling hot water, remove from heat, and let sit 10 minutes. Drain and peel tomatoes. Slice tomatoes in half horizontally, spoon out seeds, chop finely, and combine with all remaining ingredients.

Anchovy Dressing

Makes ¾ cup

1   clove garlic
1   can anchovies, packed in olive oil
3   tablespoons red wine vinegar
½   cup olive oil

Mash or puree the garlic and anchovies with their packing liquid. Mix well with vinegar and olive oil.

Spicy Island Dressing

Use this tropical dressing on mixed lettuces—butter, red romaine, watercress, arugula—topped with smoked duck or chicken. Dried cranberries and currants are nice garnish for such salads.

Makes about 1²/₃ cups

2	egg yolks
¹/₄	cup chopped ginger
1	clove garlic, chopped
2	tablespoons soy sauce
1	tablespoon white wine vinegar
1	teaspoon sesame oil
3	tablespoons honey
1	teaspoon Dijon mustard
	Juice of 2 whole limes
¹/₂	cup peanut oil
¹/₃	cup olive oil (or peanut oil)

Combine egg yolks, ginger, garlic, soy sauce, vinegar, sesame oil, honey, mustard, and lime juice in a blender and process well for a couple minutes. With blender on low speed, gradually pour peanut and olive oils in a steady stream until sauce is thickened and evenly blended. Chill for 30 minutes.

MAYONNAISE AND CREAMY DRESSINGS

Mayonnaise dressings—emulsions of egg and oil—are very rich and best for cold cooked vegetable, meat, fowl, or fish salads. The hand-beaten mayonnaise is considered the best, with its smooth satiny texture. But the blender mayonnaise can also have a pleasing fluffy consistency.

Keep in mind that these dressings take a salad from the low-calorie category to the fat-rich (and caloric), one rather quickly. Also, because of the egg, mayonnaise dressings contribute the least desirable type of fat—animal fat or a high-cholesterol one. (While vegetable oils are also fats, and thus are high-calorie, most of them add the less potentially health-threatening poly- or monounsaturated fats to your diet.) Fortunately, unless you are on a strict fat- and/or cholesterol-restricted diet, you can enjoy these dressings in small amounts, because they are also flavor-rich. You don't need an ocean of a mayonnaise dressing to enjoy it on a salad.

Basic Mayonnaise

You can use the longer hand method for any of the mayonnaise dressings. The texture will be slightly more satiny and smooth than with the quick blender method.

Makes about ³/₄ cup

1	egg
1	tablespoon fresh lemon juice
¹/₄	teaspoon minced garlic
¹/₂	teaspoon salt
¹/₂	teaspoon Dijon mustard
¹/₄	cup walnut or hazelnut oil
¹/₃	cup olive oil

Hand method: Place egg, lemon juice, garlic, salt, and mustard in the bowl and whisk until blended. Slowly add oils in a steady stream, whisking steadily until smoothly incorporated.

Blender method: Blend egg, lemon juice, garlic, salt, and mustard thoroughly. Scrape down sides of blender bowl. With blender running drizzle in the oils.

Variation: Creamy Lemon Garlic: Increase amount of lemon juice to 3 tablespoons and garlic to 1 teaspoon.

Blue Cheese Dressing

You can try different blue cheeses—Danish blue or Roquefort, for example. Gorgonzola is a mellower cheese.

Makes about 1 cup

¹/₄	cup plain yogurt
¹/₄	cup sour cream
2	tablespoons mayonnaise
¹/₄	cup crumbled gorgonzola cheese

Puree all ingredients in a blender.

Creamy Tarragon

Makes about ³/₄ cup

1	egg
2	tablespoons fresh lemon juice
1	tablespoon white wine vinegar
¹/₂	teaspoon salt
2	tablespoons chopped fresh tarragon
¹/₂	cup plus 2 tablespoons olive oil

Whirl the egg, lemon juice, vinegar, salt, and tarragon in a blender on low speed. With blender on low speed, slowly add the oil in a steady stream until smoothly incorporated.

Green Goddess Dressing

Green Goddess dressing made its debut at the Palace Hotel in San Francisco many years ago. It was reportedly concocted and named for a well-known actor of the era, who was performing in a show called The Green Goddess.

Makes about 1¹/₄ cups

²/₃   cup mayonnaise
2   anchovy fillets
3   scallions, chopped
2   tablespoons white wine vinegar
1   clove garlic, chopped
2   tablespoons fresh tarragon
3   tablespoons chopped fresh parsley
1   tablespoon chopped fresh chives
        Salt and pepper to taste

Combine all ingredients in a blender and process until smooth.

Orange Curry Mayonnaise

Makes about ³/₄ cup

1   egg
1   tablespoon white wine vinegar
2   tablespoons orange juice
1   teaspoon curry powder
¹/₂   teaspoon Dijon mustard
¹/₂   teaspoon salt
¹/₂   teaspoon grated orange peel
        Pinch of cayenne pepper
¹/₂   cup olive oil

Whirl the egg, vinegar, orange juice, curry powder, mustard, salt, orange peel, and pepper in a blender. With blender on low, slowly add oil in a steady stream until smoothly incorporated.

Cucumber Mint Dressing

On a hot summer day when you want a change of pace from heavier oil dressings, try this one. Toss it with a head of curly dark greenleaf lettuce, some ripe tomatoes, or steamed fresh green beans.

Makes 1¹/₄ cups

1   cup chopped, peeled, seedless cucumber
½   cup fresh mint leaves
½   teaspoon salt
¾   cup sour cream

Combine the cucumber, mint, and salt, and puree in a blender until the mixture is rather chunky. Pour into a bowl and stir the sour cream in by hand. Dressing will thin out too much if you puree the sour cream in the blender with the mixture.

Lemon Poppyseed Dressing

Makes about ¾ cup

1   egg
1   shallot, minced
¼   cup fresh lemon juice
½   teaspoon salt
½   teaspoon Dijon mustard
½   cup oil
1   tablespoon poppyseeds

Whirl the egg, shallot, lemon juice, salt, and mustard in a blender. With blender on low speed, slowly add the oil in a steady stream until smoothly incorporated. Add the poppyseeds and whirl quickly for 15 seconds.

Indonesian Peanut-Coconut Sauce

This dressing also has a tropical flavor with the nutty sweetness of coconut. It's great on a raw green salad of spinach, cabbage, green beans, sprouts, and cucumber. It's also good on cold chicken breast or cubes of fresh tofu.

Makes about ³/₄ cup

2	tablespoons unsalted creamy peanut butter
¹/₂	cup canned coconut milk
1	clove garlic
1	tablespoon finely chopped ginger
¹/₈	teaspoon crushed red pepper flakes
2	tablespoons lemon juice
¹/₂	teaspoon salt

Combine all ingredients in a blender and process until smooth and creamy.

Creamy Pesto Dressing

This recipe uses ingredients similar to Creamy Tarragon, page 119, but different processing makes for quite a different end result. This is virtually the same sauce you use on pasta. It's great on dark greens and tomatoes.

Makes ³/₄ cup

1	clove garlic, chopped
¹/₄	cup fresh basil or combination of basil and tarragon leaves
¹/₄	cup olive oil
¹/₂	teaspoon salt
¹/₄	cup pine nuts
¹/₄	cup finely grated parmesan cheese
¹/₃	cup half-and-half

Place the garlic, basil, and/or tarragon, olive oil, and salt in the bowl of a blender. Puree until smooth, then add nuts and puree again. Pour the sauce into a bowl and stir in the cheese and half-and-half.

NOTES

NOTES

KITCHEN METRICS

For cooking and baking convenience, the Metric Commission of Canada suggests the following for adapting to metric measurement. The table gives approximate, rather than exact, conversions.

SPOONS

¼ teaspoon	= 1	milliliter
½ teaspoon	= 2	milliliters
1 teaspoon	= 5	milliliters
1 tablespoon	= 15	milliliters
2 tablespoons	= 25	milliliters
3 tablespoons	= 50	milliliters

CUPS

¼ cup	= 50	milliliters
⅓ cup	= 75	milliliters
½ cup	= 125	milliliters
⅔ cup	= 150	milliliters
¾ cup	= 175	milliliters
1 cup	= 250	milliliters

OVEN TEMPERATURES

200°F	=	100°C
225°F	=	110°C
250°F	=	120°C
275°F	=	140°C
300°F	=	150°C
325°F	=	160°C
350°F	=	180°C
375°F	=	190°C
400°F	=	200°C
425°F	=	220°C
450°F	=	230°C
475°F	=	240°C

INDEX